EVELYN NESBIT'S OWN STORY

EVELYN NESBIT'S OWN STORY

The Death Bed Revelations Of 1926

by EVELYN NESBIT

MAIN STREET PRESS • FORT LEE, NJ

Main Street Press • *Fort Lee, NJ*

PRINTED IN THE UNITED STATES OF AMERICA

THEN, when she dropped me at 42nd street and Broadway, she leaned from the car and said simply:
"Be kind to me."

— *HARRISON HASKINS*

CONTENTS

PREFACE

— 1926

PREFACE

"EVELYN NESBIT THAW TRIES SUICIDE IN CHICAGO"

EARLY this morning, Jan. 5th, Evelyn Nesbit, formerly wife of Harry Thaw, millionaire, attempted suicide in her apartment at 56 E. Walton St., Chicago, by drinking a heavy dose of lysol. The "Broadway Butterfly" of twenty years ago, over whom Harry Thaw shot and killed Stanford White and served many years in a New York insane asylum as a result, had just completed an engagement in a Chicago cabaret and had intended journeying to Florida with her son, Russell, 15 years old. The son and a maid frantically worked in an effort to revive her, awaiting the arrival of doctors, but the actress' condition is declared to be critical. The actress herself could throw no light on the act, being in an unconscious condition. It is hinted, however, that financial difficulties may have prompted the act, as several months ago she was reported as facing bankruptcy.

* * * *

Former Stage Star To Recover, Say Physicians.

CHICAGO, Jan. 5. — Six hours after Evelyn had

swallowed the contents of an eight-ounce vial of lysol she recovered consciousness at the Ashland Boulevard Hospital and was said to have an even chance of recovery.

The once great dancer-actress, whose husband, Harry K. Thaw, spent years in a New York state insane asylum for the murder of Stanford White in one of the most dramatic triangle slayings of history, drank the poison, according to her maid, after a five-day party, during which the stage beauty incurred a fractured nose.

"This is the third time mother has attempted suicide in a period of a year," her son told Sergt. Joe Hanratty of the E. Chicago av. police. "I administered an antidote immediately. I had done that twice before and knew how."

Neighbors in the apartment building, where Evelyn occupied an elaborately furnished third-floor apartment of five rooms, said that throughout the night they were disturbed by noises of a riotous party, and the voices of several men were heard plainly.

This the maid denied, asserting that she, Miss Nesbit, as Evelyn chose to be called, and Russell were alone during the night.

It was 5 o'clock this morning when Dr. E. Thomas Brand of the Embassy Hotel, personal physician to Evelyn, was summoned to the apartment and found her unconscious on her bed, the empty lysol vial in the bathroom.

He had Evelyn removed hurriedly to Ashland Boulevard Hospital, where he and Dr. Amante Rongetti, superintendent of the hospital, made desperate effort to restore the fallen stage star to consciousness and life.

Six hours later Evelyn regained consciousness and her condition began to improve. Only the prompt administration of the antidote by her son, in the opinion of the attending physicians, had saved her life and gave her a better than even chance to recover unless complications set in.

FINISHED ENGAGEMENT

Evelyn had completed a six weeks' engagement at the Moulin Rouge cafe, 416 S. Wabash av., one of the bright night-life cabarets of the down-town district, on the Sunday after Christmas.

"Evelyn had been drinking heavily of late," the maid, Miss Gussie Accooe of Brooklyn, told police at the hospital.

"She left the house New Year's eve saying that she was going to visit some friends just outside Chicago. She did not come back until Monday morning about 5 o'clock. When she came in her nose had been broken, and she was intoxicated.

"I called a plastic surgeon who set her nose.

"She drank heavily since then. Yesterday she drank eight bottles of beer. All day and all last night she called for beer.

"About 5 o'clock this morning the beer gave out. I had been in and out of her room all night, for I was worried about her.

BROKE DRINKING GLASS

"When I told her that there was no more beer and that I could get none until the place where we obtained it was opened up this morning, she went to the bathroom. She broke a drinking glass, and I went in and picked up the pieces, because I was afraid she might cut herself with them. I saw the bottle of lysol then, but I did not think it was poison or I would have removed it. I was afraid she might harm herself.

"I took the broken glass out, and heard Evelyn call.

"I ran back and saw the empty lysol bottle in the bath tub.

"Evelyn cried out:

"'Gussie, I did it. I took lysol. I've killed myself.'

"I ran to the pantry and got a glass of milk, and took it to her. She knocked it out of my hand. Then I ran and got another, but when I got back she was unconscious on the floor.

"Russell was asleep in an alcove off the living room, and I awakened him. He kept his head and told me to call Dr. Brand."

After Dr. Brand had removed Evelyn to the hospital, Sergts. Joe Hanratty and Robert Badgley of the E. Chicago av. station, found her son alone in the apartment.

Coolly the youth asked the policemen for their credentials. When shown their stars, he appeared satisfied, but refused to answer questions.

SON TAKEN TO STATION

"I have been advised not to make any statements," he said, but refused to say who had given him the advise. Then he was taken to the E. Chicago av. station, where Lieut. E. J. Kelly endeavored to question him.

To the lieutenant he admitted that his mother had endeavored twice before to take her own life.

"I was asleep in the alcove off the living room when Gussie, the maid, awakened me," he told the lieutenant. "She said mother had taken poison. I ran to the telephone and told the operator to send a doctor and an ambulance. Then I gave mother an antidote — I had done that twice before in the last year.

"Dr. Brand and an ambulance from Scheutte's, 766 N.

Clark st., came and the doctor and I started with mother in the ambulance to the Henrotin Hospital.

"On the way Dr. Brand suggested that we go to the Ashland Blvd. Hospital instead. After we got there, I returned home and found the maid there. Then a man, whom I have seen before at the Moulin Rouge, came in and took the maid away.

"I had been at McVicker's Theater, alone, last night, returned home alone, and went to bed. I heard no commotion and did not hear anything until the maid called me."

Mrs. Ada L. Stewart, occupant of an apartment on the second floor of the building, told police that she had been kept awake by much noise in the Nesbit apartment and the loud voices of men, throughout the night, but that such was "nothing unusual."

MANY PARTIES HELD

"There have been many times when noisy parties have been held, with many men visitors present in Evelyn's apartment," Mrs. Stewart said.

Mrs. R. L. Klintich, proprietor of a dressmaking shop on the first floor, said that she was awakened about 5 a. m. by a woman's voice calling: "Russell! Russell!" She said she had not been disturbed during the night.

Closing her engagement at the Moulin Rouge, Evelyn had planned to depart tomorrow for an eight-weeks' engagement in Florida, according to the maid.

Russell had joined his mother here just before Christmas, and was to return to Atlantic City, N. J., where he attended Winchester School, a school for boys.

TREATED FOR DRUG USE

Mrs. Thaw, questioning of the maid revealed, had taken treatment at a sanitarium in New Jersey last Fall for the "dope" habit. She was released shortly before Thanksgiving, Miss Accooe, who has been her personal maid for four years, said, and appeared cured.

"I have seen no evidence of her taking drugs since," said Miss Accooe.

The physician who attended Evelyn at the hospital also was satisfied that she had not been using drugs.

"Evelyn liked Chicago," said the maid. "She had discussed the trip to Florida many times, and said that she did not like to leave Chicago.

"She has had many admirers during the four years that I have been with her, but I do not know of anyone who might be called a particular sweetheart. All that she seemed to live for was her son."

Russell appeared cool, collected.

DRUG LETTER SEIZED

A cryptic letter found in Miss Nesbit's apartment signed "Dr. R.," postmarked Brownsville, Pa., Jan. 1, and beginning "Dearest Eve," was seized by the police for inquiry.

"Dam narcotic gang were pushing me for the $150," it ran, "but had to meet a truckload almost of obligations and could not connect up with friends here or Pittsburgh — only have a limited time to send on cash — banks and everything would be closed Christmas Day — (got panicky). Thought Al might give me a lift for a hundred — wired him — no answer."

Another letter beginning "Dear Florence" and signed

"Mama," evidently written to Miss Nesbit, was mailed at Pittsburgh December 30. It indicated that Evelyn had been having trouble with her throat and teeth.

At 10:30 a. m. Miss Nesbit became semi-conscious and began calling for "Alice." The doctor and nurses did not know to whom she referred. Emetics and the use of the stomach pump, her physician believed, had removed most of the poison, and her return to partial consciousness gave hope that she would recover.

SON REFUSED TO TALK

When Sergts. Joe Hanratty and Robert Badgley of the E. Chicago av. police first appeared at the apartment, he demanded to be shown their credentials. He appeared satisfied when shown their stars, but refused point-blank to answer any and all questions. He would not even give his name or his age.

He said that he had "been advised not to make any statements," but who had given the advice he refused to say.

The writing desk in the living room of Evelyn's apartment was piled high with Christmas and New Year's cards, telegrams and letters of well wishes, from admirers and friends all over the country.

On the piano in the living room were many favorite songs of the ill-fated little dancer who twenty years ago was the toast of Broadway. Most of them bore the inscription: "Evelyn Nesbit."

On the dining room table were the remains of a meal, the evening meal of last night, according to the maid, which she had not had time to remove because of the demands of her mistress for attention.

BEDROOM IN DISORDER

Except for the dining room and Evelyn's bedroom, which were in disorder, the rest of the apartment was clean and neat.

"There is no chance of the poisoning having been accidental," Dr. Rongetti said after a thorough examination. "No one could drink eight ounces of lysol accidentally."

Evelyn had been playing the role of chief entertainer at the Moulin Rouge for six weeks and had made a previous appearance there last May.

*   *   *   *

"N.J. FRIENDS SURPRISED"

ATLANTIC CITY, N.J., Jan. 5. — Friends of Evelyn Nesbit Thaw expressed surprise today over the news that she had tried to commit suicide in Chicago. When she left here late in October, at the end of the Summer season in the cabarets, she was reported in good health and well-to-do financially.

When she came to Atlantic City to make her home three years ago her health was poor. Finally, she recuperated, and went into the cabaret business, where she displayed ability as a singer and as an owner. At various times she managed several cabarets and night clubs. She is also reputed to have made considerable money in the real estate business.

Last Summer it was reported that Harry Thaw was coming to Atlantic City to provide for her and her son, Russell. Thaw's lawyer wrote to her and she made arrangements to buy a $40,000 home on the strength of the communication. The story was given publication and Thaw decided not to come.

Just before she went to Chicago she had planned to sing

in Florida. She changed her plans on receipt of a warning that the Ku Klux Klan would not tolerate her presence in that State.

*   *   *   *

"EVELYN NESBIT STILL IN DANGER"

Complications Follow Her Attempt at Suicide.

THROAT BURNED BY POISON

Ex-Wife of Harry Thaw Glad She Did Not Die.

CHICAGO, Jan. 6 (A. P.). — Evelyn Nesbit Thaw was suffering to-day from complications that followed her suicide effort yesterday when she drank eight ounces of poison. Physicians said she might recover with several days of hard fighting, but expressed themselves as not ready to state she was out of danger.

Her burned throat gave considerable trouble and she could not talk.

Russell Thaw, her 15-year-old son, remained here to-day, his return to school at Atlantic City having been postponed.

Miss Nesbit last night declared she was glad the poison did not kill her.

"Life looked hopeless. Now it looks promising and colorful," she told Dr. E. Thomas Brand, her physician. The alcohol in the liquors she had been drinking for several days was a natural antidote for the poison she used.

"I took the stuff," she said after recovering consciousness, "because I was 'blue,' I thought life had given me more of its rough edges than I deserved. It was only on an impulse that I took poison."

PARTY IN APARTMENT DENIED

Glad, too, that she will not die is Russell, who poured olive oil and milk down her throat as antidotes after she had drained the poison bottle. He left the hospital last night after physicians had assured him his mother was out of danger, but cautioned him against seeing her for a day.

Beyond her statement to Dr. Brand, no motive was assigned for the suicide attempt, which was her second. Russell and Gussie Accooe, her maid, both denied that there had been a party in the apartment before she took the poison. The maid admitted that the divorced wife of Harry K. Thaw had been drinking heavily since New Year's and had returned home Monday with a broken nose.

Friends, recalling that she no longer appeared as a singer in a south side cabaret, thought of financial troubles, but from Pittsburgh came despatches to Chicago papers quoting Harry Thaw as saying he was sending her $10 a day and had sent her $310 December 31.

LITTLE GLEANED FROM LETTERS

No information was gleaned from two letters found in her room. Two signed "Mama" referred to financial affairs and appeared to be from Mrs. C. J. Holman of Pittsburgh, Evelyn's mother.

Another signed "Doc R.," and addressing her as "Dear Eve," made references to a narcotic gang "pushing me for $150," and "will be much disappointed if within a few days I do not hear from you." At Brownsville, Pa., Dr. W. Calvin Roller said the $150 meant the payment of a fine and added that he had met Evelyn in a sanitarium where she was taking treatment.

*   *   *   *

"EVELYN THAW'S SUICIDE ATTEMPT EXPLAINED"

Harry's Ex-Wife Feared Dying of Draught in West

Atlantic City Dancer Blamed for Despair That Led to Her Taking Poison.

NEW YORK, Jan. 6. — Jealousy of Evelyn Nesbit Thaw's "come-back" from the drug habit and of her restored beauty and social success drove the former wife of Harry Thaw from Atlantic City and a successful business, placed her at death's door through her frantic attempt to kill herself yesterday and caused Russell, her faithful son, to be arrested.

A man who knows his Broadway and the thrust and counter-thrust of intrigue that goes on among women favorites of men just beyond the arc of the White Lights, pronounced Evelyn Nesbit Thaw the victim of another woman. And the other woman, he said, is Evan Burrows Fontaine, herself, an announced victim of Cornelius Vanderbilt (Sonny) Whitney.

Young Russell Thaw was taken into custody yesterday afternoon by the Chicago police when he point-blank refused to answer any questions regarding the attempted suicide of his mother in their apartment at No. 56 Walton Pl.

Evelyn Nesbit made

THE THIRD ATTEMPT

to take her life early yesterday morning. It was at 5 o'clock that the boy, spending his holidays from Winchester School, was awakened by her groans and found her lying in her night clothes in the bathroom.

Gussie Accooe, of Brooklyn, Miss Nesbit's maid for the last four years, said the Broadway favorite of 20 years ago had swallowed half a pint of acid disinfectant.

Miss Nesbit, she said, had been despondent for several days and had been drinking a great deal. She came home early Monday morning quite intoxicated. She went to bed but did not stay there. She wanted something to drink and became angry when she could find only eight bottles of beer in the house. As the day and the night wore on, her nervousness increased, it was said. In the small hours she went alone to the bathroom and drank the acid.

At the Ashland Boulevard Hospital, it was said her condition was very serious and her recovery doubtful.

In Atlantic City, her friends

EXPRESSED SURPRISE

at her attempt to commit suicide. When she left there last October at the end of the Summer season of the cabarets, she was in good health and well-to-do financially.

When she went there three years ago her health was low. She was in the grip of the drug habit. But she fought back in a sanitarium. She went into the cabaret business. She displayed ability both as a singer and an owner. At various times, she managed several cabarets and night clubs and she was reputed to have made quite a sum in real estate.

All this is true, admits the man who knows his Broadway, but under the surface, under the lights of Evelyn

Nesbit Thaw's successful cabarets, there burned Evan Burrows Fontaine's jealousy.

Evan Burrows Fontaine also has

A LITTLE SON

whom she adores. This little son was the main reason for one of the *causes celebres* in American legal history. Miss Fontaine has sued Sonny Whitney repeatedly, charging he was the father of the child.

Now Evan Burrows Fontaine lives in a cottage in Atlantic City.

And just across the way from the little cottage is a stable inhabited by a gorgeous white pony that the baby rides. He loves the little animal so much that he insists on looking at him as soon as he gets up in the morning.

Now, one would think that satisfied mother love would turn a woman sweet. But Evan Burrows Fontaine felt the enmity that is ever present in women toward other women. The name of Evelyn Nesbit Thaw was being constantly dinned in her ears. Evelyn's case was more celebrated than her own attempt to wrest $1,000,000 from a powerful American family. Evelyn Thaw had "come back" from the shadows of the drug habit. Evelyn Thaw was a good singer and a good ball-room dancer. She was also a good business woman.

So Evan Burrows Fontaine writhed. And when she writhed she did it to some purpose because she was a protegee of a

"BIG MAN."

When you go into Atlantic City wanting anything involving large sums of money, you must see Enoch L. (Nucky)

Johnson. He is County Leader. He is everything in the watering resort. He is "The Man You See." He is — or was — a fervent admirer of Evan Fontaine, until she was supplanted in his affections by a wee dancer.

It was at the time his affections were at their height that Evan writhed to her greatest purpose. She had recently been tossed out of "The Silver Slipper," one of Atlantic City's highest class cabarets. And she had been superseded by Evelyn Nesbit who was throwing her costumes after her when the Fontaine woman attacked her with her claws. The fight, spectators say, was a fight.

It wasn't long after this that Evelyn Thaw, by underground wire, received orders to

"GET OUT."

She got out, but it broke her heart.

The person behind Miss Nesbit's orders to move on and quit Atlantic City was Evan Burrows Fontaine, says the Man Who Knows His Broadway. Now, her baby rides about on his little pony and his mother reclines in her late bed, purring contentedly at the removal of her great rival. Of course, there is the wee dancer. But one can't have everything.

Evelyn Nesbit Thaw recovered consciousness late yesterday. She is in great pain.

When informed in Pittsburgh that his divorced wife had attempted suicide, Harry K. Thaw, visiting his aged mother, showed deep concern.

"I hope she will quickly recover," he said. "I am very sorry. Something over a year ago there was an interruption but since last July she receives $10 a day and I believe she earned much more from her theatrical entertainment. Three hundred dollars was mailed Dec. 31 last. I do hope she gets better."

Miss Nesbit was completing an engagement in Chicago when she took the poison. She was to have gone to Florida today.

*   *   *   *

"EVELYN HAS RELAPSE"

New Turn Brings Fear of Strangulation from Burns of Acid, but Doctors Hopeful for Recovery.

CHICAGO, Jan. 7. — Evelyn Nesbit Thaw suffered a relapse yesterday afternoon and may die from strangulation caused by the burning away of the lining of her throat by the acid disinfectant she took.

The release came shortly after 3 o'clock. Her temperature rose rapidly and stood at 100.8. Fears of complications, indicated by the increase in temperature, were voiced by Drs. E. Thomas Brand and Amante Rongetti.

Though the physicians admitted early today that Miss Nesbit's condition was serious, they held high hopes for her recovery. Strychnine was given in a series of injections to give her strength to bear the pain of burns in her throat caused by the eight ounces of poison she had drunk.

The large quantity of gin she had drunk during the party at which she suffered a broken nose, neutralized the effects of the poison she had taken in an effort to end her life, it was reported.

In the shadow of death, Miss Nesbit begged her doctors to help her to another chance to live.

"I don't want to die now," she told them weakly. "I wanted to die yesterday when I realized what a hell of a life was mine. But I want to live now. I want another chance. Life is better than I thought. But this pain is terrible."

Asked why she tried to end her life, the former model, stage star and wife of Harry K. Thaw, replied:

"I was full of gin, beer and whisky and just drank it. I drank plenty in hopes that it would be enough."

* * * *

"EVELYN THAW IN DEATH SHADOW"

CHICAGO, Jan. 7. — Evelyn Nesbit's life still hangs in the balance.

Tossing in agony from the acid burns of the poison she took at the end of a five-day drinking bout, the former wife of Harry K. Thaw began the uphill battle to regain her shattered health.

Her vocal chords have been temporarily paralyzed by the action of the powerful disinfectant which she swallowed, and her temperature hovered about the 100 degree mark while her pulse raced to 130. It was the reaction that had set in, not only of the poison but of the poisonous alcohol she consumed.

There was, however, a hopeful factor on which Dr. E. Thomas Brand, her attending physician, was able to base a more optimistic prediction.

"Miss Nesbit wants to live," said Dr. Brand. "She no longer looks on life as hopeless as she did when she took the poison.

"She is worse than I expected to find her, however, and is far from being out of danger. Her entire throat, stomach, intestines and even the back of her nose are terribly burned. She has lost her voice and suffers intense pain. No one, except her son, will be admitted to the sickroom.

"There are two chief dangers she now faces — strangulation from contraction of the throat because of the acid burns and inflammation of the kidneys. It will be several days before we can say definitely that she is out of danger, and it will be weeks before she is completely recovered,"

Russell Thaw, the dancer's fifteen-year-old son, was at his mother's bedside most of the day.

* * * *

"EVELYN NESBIT PASSES CRISIS; WILL RECOVER"

CHICAGO, Jan. 7. — Evelyn Nesbit passed the crisis in her battle for life early today. Suffering a relapse between 4 and 6 o'clock yesterday, in which her life was despaired of, the dancer rallied against the overwhelming odds of self-administered poison.

Her physicians, who had been called into consultation when her pulse mounted out of all proportion to her temperature, are again optimistic of the outcome.

"Miss Nesbit will recover, but it will be a long fight before she fully regains her health," said Dr. E. Thomas Brand. "In a week she may be convalescent enough to permit her removal from the hospital. But she will require careful nursing for some weeks."

Among the scores of telegrams which arrived at the hospital was one from a Los Angeles cabaret manager, who offered her an extended engagement.

Dr. Brand replied to the telegram stating that the dancer

would be able to fulfill it, but he could set no definite date for his patient.

Her voice will be temporarily impaired due to injuries to her vocal cords from the powerful disinfectant which she swallowed. Physicians however, doubted that she had swallowed eight ounces of the poison as had first been believed.

An inflammation of the skin, due to the poison's action, as well as the alcohol she had consumed in her four-day drinking bout, made the dancer uncomfortable, but when the eruption subsided she fell into a peaceful slumber.

Her son, Russell, was permitted to talk to her for a few minutes. He embraced his mother and received her whispered words of affection.

* * * *

"MISS NESBIT THREATENS TO TRY SUICIDE AGAIN WHEN SHE GETS WELL, DECLARING SHE IS TIRED OF LIVING"

CHICAGO, Jan. 8. — Evelyn Nesbit Thaw plans to die by her own hand just as soon as she gets out of the hospital, where she is now recovering from her third suicide attempt.

She's "simply sick of living," she told Dr. Amante Rongetti, head of the hospital, when he sought to assure her yesterday she soon would be well.

"You might as well let me die," she retorted. "I don't want to get well. If I get well I'll do it again, anyhow, and do it with something deadlier than acid. More, I'll do it where no one will find me and give me an antidote."

As a result of her threat she will be kept constantly under

the eye of a nurse while in the hospital.

* * * *

"PEACE TALK OF EVELYN AND THAW"

Harry's Impending Chicago Trip and Money Gifts Stir Reconciliation Rumor.

CHICAGO, Jan. 8. — Evelyn Nesbit, who is recovering from a suicide attempt, learned today that her former husband, Harry K. Thaw, is coming here next week.

While Thaw is said to be coming to confer with his attorney, Charles S. Wharton, his visit at this time, coupled with his recent concern over the welfare of the woman for whom he killed Stanford White twenty years ago, has given rise to rumors of a reconciliation. Thaw's continued sending of $10 a day to Evelyn, is taken as further proof of his interest in her.

Thaw has been keeping track of Evelyn's movements for some time, through a firm of private detectives, it was learned. Immediately after Evelyn was taken to the hospital, he telephoned to a detective in his employ to visit the hospital and give him a report on Evelyn's condition.

Evelyn, whose relapse caused some concern after her recent attempt to end her life, has passed the crisis, but she "lacks the will to live" according to doctors.

The dancer said she felt "blue" when told that she would live, adding that she hoped she wouldn't "get well and have to face the whole thing over again."

* * * *

"HARRY THAW RETURNS TO LITTLE VILLAGE DANCER"

Shows Jealousy as Girl Gets Too Many Phone Calls

Sends Flowers and Money in Strange Letter to Her — Greets Pals in Night Clubs.

NEW YORK, Jan. 9. — Harry K. Thaw, who disappeared from Pittsburgh so mysteriously and suddenly that it was reported he had gone to the bedside of Evelyn Nesbit, his former wife, in Chicago, is in New York to continue his gay life.

Up to date, he has been extremely busy. On Thursday afternoon he had a two-hour *tete-a-tete* with Miss Kitty Mulligan, a dancer at "Jimmie" Kelly's place on Sullivan St. On Thursday night he was almost mobbed by actresses and other fashionable women at Texas Guinan's 300 Club.

Thaw arrived in New York at 11 o'clock Thursday and went directly to the Hotel Roosevelt, his regular stopping place. The Roosevelt was full and he went to the Belmont, where he was given Room 401.

He called on an aged friend of his mother's at the Hotel Bossert, Brooklyn, and on his physician, Dr. Sello, 52d St. and 9th Ave.

CALLS UP EVELYN

At 2 o'clock in the afternoon he was calling the Ashland Hotel in Chicago to inquire as to Evelyn Nesbit's condition.

His first act on getting into New York was to call Miss Mulligan on the telephone. Madge Wilcox, who shares her apartment with her, told him Miss Mulligan was asleep and could not be disturbed.

A half hour later a uniformed messenger arrived with a huge bouquet of American beauty roses for Miss Mulligan. The envelope accompanying them contained $10 and a note addressed to "Miss Mulligan's girl friend."

LETTER TO GIRL

"Please give these to her and please do not worry, *it read.*
"Here's the $10, ½ for you and the rest for a splendid breakfast right off.

"Then tell her to be all ready at 2½ to 3½. She knows, for he was able to go to her grand-mother's in Allentown. Yours truly."

Miss Mulligan climbed wearily from her bed. She had not kept a promise she had made Thaw over the telephone to get in touch with him over the Christmas holidays while she was on a visit to Allentown, Pa. She had received this letter of protest from him:

"Not one word from you. So I'm writing. It will be this week, not later. Please write at once so that I can address a letter to your apartment.

"Then, when I know the day, you could tell Mr. Kelly and he could ask Mr. O. But most likely

I could see you earlier that day
and tell me if noon is all right, if
I am there Thursday.   Sincerely."

LETTER UNSIGNED

There was no name signed to either the letter or the note, because Harry K. Thaw never signs his name to any of his letters to women friends.

He arrived at Miss Mulligan's apartment at 2:45 Thursday afternoon and he spent three hours talking to her. He told her of his ex-wife's attempt to commit suicide and also how sorry he was for her and how earnestly he hoped that she would recover. He left in a rage because Miss Mulligan got too many telephone calls while he was visiting her.

Thursday night he went to see "The Princess Flavia" at the Century Theatre and there lost a handkerchief. He said it was a woman's handkerchief. And he spent more than an hour, aided by the entire staff of the theatre, in an unsuccessful effort to find it.

He reached Texas Guinan's "300 Club" at about 1 o'clock yesterday morning, and was greeted uproariously by the crowd there.

HOPES FOR EVELYN

Thaw spoke with a great deal of feeling when he told his questioners that she was recovering. He added that he hoped she would be fully recovered soon.

Among those who greeted him were Sadie Brent, George Whiting, Sir Robert Peel, Beatrice Lille, Carl Hysen and Peggy Harris.

Frances Williams, a night club dancer and a tall and

willowy blonde, did a Charleston for Thaw, who viewed her performance with the deepest gravity.

He also watched carefully the dancing of Ruby Keeler and Mary Lucas, two performers in Texas Guinan's mob. He was very attentive as Texas gathered her mob around his table and told a bedtime story of "The Little Boy Who Beat the Bunnies," and learned they could not add, not alone multiply, as the teacher told them they could.

In Chicago, Evelyn Nesbit, believing her ex-husband was on his way to see her, said she did not believe she could stand the excitement of seeing him at this time.

She left the hospital yesterday.

* * * *

"DOPE RING VENGEANCE HINT IN NESBIT CASE"

Evelyn's Friends to Direct Detectives To Clear Poisoning.

NEW YORK, Jan. 9. — Was the poison swallowed by Evelyn Nesbit, divorced wife of Harry K. Thaw, eccentric millionaire, self-administered or part of a diabolical scheme of the Chicago underworld and drug ring to "get" her for turning reformer and "squealer"?

This question is agitating friends of the dancer in all parts of the country. Her coterie of night life adherents in Atlantic City, N. J., believe she was poisoned and are backing their contentions by hiring detectives.

These sleuths will go to Chicago where she is convalescing and they will conduct a thorough investigation.

In Atlantic City, spokesmen for the underworld stated the dancer had earned the enmity of the Chicago drug ring. This was due to her activities to prevent young girls using dope. Part of her plans, it is said, was to expose venders of deadly narcotics.

It was also stated that she was contemplating starting a national drive against the sale and use of drugs. To do this she was scheduled to turn over to government authorities a mass of evidence she has collected.

But the sporting fraternity in Atlantic City wants Evelyn to return there. They are so confident she will recover they are making plans to provide for her and her son, Russell.

An ocean front apartment has been rented for her use. Funds are also being raised to defray any expenses she might have incurred while in Chicago and en route there.

* * * *

"THAW TO AID EVELYN ONLY"

Beyond Providing Her With Money He Is Through, He Asserts.

NEW YORK, Jan. 9. — Harry K. Thaw himself today definitely declared himself concerning his future relations with Evelyn Nesbit, his former wife, who is recovering in Chicago after a third attempt to end her life. A reconciliation between them had been anticipated because of a reported trip to Chicago which Thaw never took.

The white-haired slayer of Stanford White, who is staying at the Hotel Belmont, said Evelyn apparently had "made a mess of her life," and that he would be always willing to help her with money, but beyond that he was "through."

"I shall always be ready to help her with money and see that she gets on her feet again," he said, "but to say that I am going back to the woman who is responsible for wrecking my life — well that's all nonsense. That's all moonshine."

Thaw, who arrived in New York Thursday, spent what was for him a quiet evening last night. Accompanied by a married couple from Pittsburgh, he went to "Charlot's Revue" and applauded vigorously the mimicry of Beatrice Lille. After the show he went to the 300 Club, on Fifty-fourth street near Seventh avenue where he greeted Texas Guinan warmly. "Tex" is the hostess who introduced Thaw to Fawn Gray, the dancer, whom he is said to have showered with gifts.

"Why should I go to Chicago?" he asked. "Mrs. Holman, Evelyn's mother, who lives in Pittsburgh, knows of her illness and doubtless will go to see her. But as far as anything between Evelyn and me now — the book is closed. As long as she lives though, I'll see that she doesn't want for the bare necessities of life or the little luxuries that I can give her.

WHY HE CAME HERE

"More than two years ago she tried to end her life here in New York. At that time financial difficulties were the cause. This last episode I know nothing about except what I have read in the newspapers.

"Frankly, I'll tell you why I came to New York, I came to see Dr. James Russell, a specialist. My mother is ill in Pittsburgh. She is eighty-four and has arterial trouble. Dr. Russell has been recommended to me and I have come to see him, in the hope that he can benefit her. I also expect to see my own doctor."

*　　*　　*　　*

"HARRY THAW ON VISIT HERE TO AID MOTHER"

NEW YORK, Jan. 9. (*Evening Edition*) — Harry K. Thaw, at his room in the Hotel Belmont today, reiterated his statement that he intends to help, financially, Evelyn Nesbit Thaw, who is recovering in Chicago after a third attempt to end her life, but he emphatically declared that he would never go back to her.

Asked about a two-hour *tete-a-tete* he was reported in morning papers to have had with Miss Kitty Mulligan, a dancer at "Jimmie" Kelly's cabaret on Sullivan street, Thaw denied knowing the girl.

"She's a new one on me," he said. "I never heard of her. No merit to the story, young man, no merit to the story. Someone is looking for a little cheap advertising."

The conversation was between Thaw, who was in his bed and an Evening Journal reporter who was in the lobby of the hotel. The reporter asked Thaw if he would pose for a picture and Harry with a wild chuckle replied:

"Wait until I go to Pittsburgh and get my hair cut by my own barber, and I'll pose for a picture for you."

SEEKS MEDICAL ADVISE

He said he was going to confer with two physicians regarding his mother and himself. He will see Dr. James Russell, a specialist, about his mother, and another physician, his private one, about himself.

Dr. Russell is the physician who attended Earle Sande, the famous jockey, after Sande was nearly killed in a spill at Saratoga a year ago. At that time it was predicted that Sande would never ride again, but today Sande is as good as ever.

Thaw said his mother, who is now eighty-four, has arterial trouble, and that Dr. Russell was recommended to him.

Questioned about a report that he intended to go back to Evelyn, the white-haired slayer of Stanford White said that she had "made a mess" of her life and that he would always be ready to help her with money, but beyond that he was through.

"WRECKED MY LIFE"

"I shall always be ready to help her with money and see that she gets on her feet again," he said, "but to say that I am going back to the woman who is responsible for wrecking my life — well that's all nonsense. That's all moonshine."

Thaw, who arrived in New York Thursday, spent what was for him a quiet evening last night. Accompanied by a married couple from Pittsburgh, he went to "Charlot's Revue" and applauded vigorously the mimicry of Beatrice Lille. After the show he went to the 300 Club, on Fifty-fourth street near Seventh avenue where he greeted Texas Guinan warmly. "Tex" is the hostess who introduced Thaw to Fawn Gray, the dancer, whom he is said to have showered with gifts.

*   *   *   *

"THAW REFUSES TO SEE EVELYN"

NEW YORK, Jan. 10. — Harry K. Thaw is not going to see Evelyn Nesbit Thaw, and he is not considering reconciliation with his former wife. A statement as to his interest in and further relations with the former show girl, who is recovering from an attempt to commit suicide, was made last night by Thaw at his hotel. He said:

"I never had any intention of going to Chicago to see

Evelyn. I am going to keep on sending her money, of course. — the regular $10 a day — but anything else is out of the question."

Thaw claimed that the sole purpose of his present trip here was to see his physician. He said he intended to leave soon for Pittsburgh to see his mother, who is ill there.

In the meanwhile, Evelyn Nesbit last night signed a contract to appear in a stock burlesque theatre in New York for the remainder of the season. Her salary was reported as $500 a week. And she has promised to be a good girl from now on. She wired:

"This time I am off drink for good. I've got to get down to hard work. I'm going to be a good girl from now on."

*   *   *   *

"FRIENDS TO AID EVELYN NESBIT"

ATLANTIC CITY, N. J., Jan. 11. — Friends of Evelyn Nesbit, former wife of Harry K. Thaw, were reported to be collecting a fund here to enable the dancer to open a new night club in Atlantic City. The movement was started when Evelyn Nesbit recently attempted suicide in Chicago.

The persons in back of the movement are to bring Miss Nesbit back to Atlantic City as soon as her condition permits, and according to reports, will clear her of all debt. Later, it was said, they will establish the new night club for her at this resort.

*   *   *   *

"FRIENDS TO GIVE EVELYN NEW CHANCE"

ATLANTIC CITY, N. J., Jan. 11. — If Evelyn Nesbit will not try to commit suicide again friends here say they will raise funds to free her from debt, and to establish her in a new night club, all her own.

These friends say that as soon as the former wife of Harry K. Thaw recovers sufficiently from her last suicidal attempt they will bring her back to Atlantic City and "give her a chance to make good."

*　*　*　*

"HOSPITAL GUARDED AGAINST REPORTED VISIT OF THAW"

CHICAGO, Jan. 11. — A report from Pittsburgh today that Harry K. Thaw had left for Chicago caused excitement at the West Side Hospital where Evelyn Nesbit Thaw is recovering from an attempt at suicide.

The hospital was guarded against a surprise appearance of the actress' former husband but the guard was withdrawn when Pittsburgh reported that Thaw had not gone West as reported earlier in the day.

*　*　*　*

"EVELYN IS SUED FOR $3,000"

ATLANTIC CITY, N. J., Jan. 13. — Suits aggregating nearly $3,000 for work done in connection with the erecting of her home here have been brought in the courthouse at Mays Landing against Evelyn Nesbit Thaw, now recovering from the effects of poison in Chicago.

The complaints are the Somers Lumber Company and Jacob S. Hyman, contractor. Miss Nesbit is said to maintain that she does not own the house. Friends here are collecting a fund to clear Miss Nesbit of debt and reinstate her in a local cabaret.

*   *   *   *

"EVELYN NESBIT FLOUTS RIVAL"

CHICAGO, Jan. 13. — Fawn Gray, Broadway dancer, got the cold shoulder when she went calling on Evelyn Nesbit Thaw today at the hospital where the latter is still a patient as the result of her suicide attempt last week.

Miss Gray, whose name was linked with that of Harry K. Thaw, Miss Nesbit's divorced husband, and who came here to succeed her as entertainer at a cabaret, got as far as the hospital office. Then she got this message:

"Miss Nesbit will not see you."

Miss Gray laid down a huge bouquet of roses she had brought and asked that they be given to some friendless patient, saying:

"I'm hurt that she feels that way, but Miss Nesbit is her own guide."

*   *   *   *

JANUARY 1926

Sunday	Monday	Tuesday	Wednesday	Thursday	Friday	Saturday
					1 New Years Day	2
3	4 After a prolonged New Year's Eve party, Evelyn returns home at 5:00 a. m. intoxicated.	5 Evelyn Nesbit tries suicide in Chicago, at about 5:00 a. m. by drinking lysol.	6	7 Harry K. Thaw arrives in New York City, not Chicago as expected.	8 Evelyn leaves Ashland Blvd. Hospital and goes to West Side Hospital in Chicago.	9
10	11 West Side Hospital on guard against rumored visit from Harry Thaw. The guard is later lifted.	12	13 Fawn Gray barred from seeing Evelyn at West Side Hospital.	14	15	16
17	18	19	20	21	22	23
24/31	25	26	27	28	29	30

Calendar Of Events

October 1925. Evelyn Nesbit Thaw when she arrived in Chicago from Atlantic City, N. J. for her present engagement.

PHOTO SHOWS an exterior view of apartments at 56 E. Walton St., and in the third floor of which Miss Nesbit attempted suicide in her suite.

The Chicago American

VOL. XXVI., NO. 166—P. M.   CHICAGO, TUESDAY, JANUARY 5, 1926.   PRICE THREE CENTS.

PHOTOS

Photos tell the story and often tell it better than words. You will note that The Chicago Evening American's news pages are always attractively and pointedly illustrated with newsy pictures.

ROBERT SCOTT TO BE RETURNED HERE

CHICAGO STUDENT DROWNED IN POOL AT U. OF I.

EVELYN THAW TRIES POISON DEATH

Princess on Way to Carol

Fighting to Bring Evelyn Thaw Back to Life

MAN HELD IN WEST AS ROBERT SCOTT TO BE RETURNED HERE

John Redding, identified in California as Robert Scott, holder of the State's bullet, Russell Scott, will be brought back to Chicago to confront witnesses of the killing of Joseph B. Maus, clerk in the City Hall pharmacy, who was shot in the back early in April, 1924.

Scott communicated with Califon and police regarding the movements of the lad made into little known, but the police held that Scott was the man who shot the pharmacy clerk.

FORMER STAGE STAR TO RECOVER, SAY PHYSICIANS

Evelyn Nesbit Thaw, the Broadway butterfly of twenty years ago, attempted to take her own life by drinking poison in her apartment at 56 E. Walton place early today.

Only prompt action by her 15-year-old son, Russell, who administered an antidote, saved her life.

Five hours after she had swallowed the contents of an eight-ounce vial of lysol she recovered consciousness in the Ashland Boulevard Hospital and was said to have a...

Evelyn Nesbit Thaw, the Broadway butterfly of twenty years ago, attempted to take her own life by drinking poison in her apartment at 55 E. Wal-ton place early today.

Only prompt action by her 15-year-old son, Russell, who administered an antidote, saved her life.

Six hours after Evelyn had swallowed the contents of an eight-ounce vial of lysol she recovered consciousness at the Ashland Boulevard Hospital and was said to have an even chance of recovery.

The same gross demonstrations...

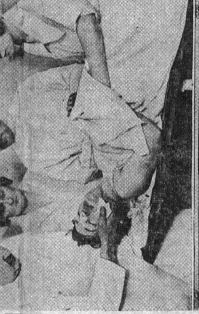

VERY LATEST NEWS

THURMAN ROBBERS FLEE TO GRAND JURY

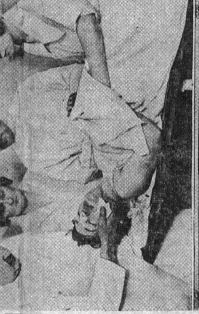

EVELYN THAW LONG SOUGHT HAPPINESS

"I'll follow the rainbow trail to the end of the rainbow, for the end of the rainbow is the pot of happiness that inclose for, as justice's balancing measure for the trouble and trials that have been mine since that night of terror years ago. What I'm convinced that there is no pot of happiness at the end of the rainbow I'll try some other trail."

Continued on Page 6, Column 1.

Continued on Page 7, Column 1.

MARCUS LOEW HERE TO SEE 'BIG PARADE'

THE WEATHER

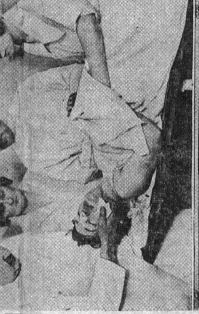

DR. BRAND.

NURSE GLYNN.

DR. RONGETTI.

NURSE LUCAS.

The story in the picture, from left to right, are Dr. E. Thomas Brand, Miss Glynn, nurse; Dr. Amueri Rongetti and Estella De Lucas, nurse. Photo by Chicago Evening American staff photographer.

Photo shows desperate fight being made at Ashland Boulevard Hospital to save the life of Evelyn Nesbit Thaw, who was found early Friday unconscious from poison. Evelyn is shown on the operating table. Note her swollen lips, from the burns caused by the poison.

CHICAGO YOUTH DROWNED AT U. OF I.

CAROL QUIT THRONE AS POLITICAL MOVE

EX-SCOTLAND YARD CHIEF IS CONVICTED

MARY M'CORMACK VERY ILL AT NICE

PURE MILK SUPPLY FOR CHICAGO FOUND

Your 1926 Resolution

EVELYN NESBIT BITTER ❖ AS TIME FAILS ❖ TO THAW HER WOES

ARTISTS MODEL

Here is Evelyn Nesbit, herself once a Greenwich Village artist's model, her marvelous worth sought anew because of her beauty.

All photos except one at left by Chicago Evening American staff photographers.

CHICAGO HOME.

Here is the studio at 66 E. Walton place, where Evelyn made her home with her son and a maid. The hunt shows the studio atmosphere in which Evelyn has spent her life.

THE BOY.

Russell Thaw, Evelyn's son, born in Paris seventeen years ago. For his sake she has waged a fight to determine his legitimacy.

RECENT.

Evelyn Nesbit Thaw as she appeared in recent weeks as an entertainer and hostess at her own Café. She was principally a singer.

HER HOME.

This is the exterior of the Evelyn Nesbit Thaw home at 66 E. Walton Café. It was here the famed woman tried to end her life.

CLOSE-UP.

And here is a good close-up view of Evelyn's face. Even today, after the tragedy, traces of the girlish placidity from her teens.

EVELYN NESBIT TRIES TO END LIFE BY POISON

Evelyn's Life-Long Search for Peace From Tragedy

SWORE TO FOLLOW RAINBOW ON HAPPINESS TRAIL

Treated for Drug Use

Son Taken to Station

Finished Engagement

Son Refused to Talk

HER POPULARITY GROWS.

Saved From Chair

Divorced in 1915

Seeks Sage Farms

WHEN BROADWAY ADORED EVELYN :: HOW TIME HAS DEALT WITH HER AND HARRY

YEARS AGO.

This is Evelyn many years ago, when Broadway toasted her and sought the company as a beautiful model.

BUTTERFLY.

Here is another photo of Evelyn Nesbit, when Thaw and Stanford White were leaders of the race for the favor.

BEFORE AND AFTER.

Harry K. Thaw was a vigorous young man in his early thirties, as shown at the left here. At the right he is seen as an older man, stamped by years in an insane asylum and by haunting thoughts.

AFTER THE TRIAL.

Evelyn Nesbit is shown here as she looked after the murder trial had ended and she had begun her fight against fate.

Chicago Evening American

Returns Home

Attack Child's Name

Big Ordeal Begins

Shot Three Times

Seeks Stage Fame

Son Refused to Talk

Many Parties Held

Broke Drinking Glass

RAINBOW?

FADING.

Tragic Highlights in the Eventful Life of Evelyn Nesbit Thaw

MAD WITH JEALOUSY, Harry K. Thaw kills Stanford White, famous architect, on the old Madison Square Garden roof in June, 1906. The crime is enacted just 14 months after the young millionaire had wed Evelyn Nesbit following a hectic wooing.

AT AMAZING TRIAL of Thaw, alleged confessions of Evelyn as to intimacies with White are repeated on the witness stand. The slayer is committed to Matteawan. Evelyn is divorced and soon after gives birth to a baby boy, Russell, whom she declares is Thaw's son.

A "COME-BACK" is staged by Evelyn when she opens a successful cabaret in Atlantic City. She, ill-starred disciple of the gay life, draws throngs to the merry rendezvous. And her success wins the undying enmity of Evan Burrows Fontaine, so it is said.

THIRD SUICIDE TRY comes as a result of the feud between Evelyn and Evan. The former had been driven from Atlantic City as a sequence to a hair-pulling match. Despondent after a prolonged New Year's celebration, Evelyn takes poison in Chicago.

DEATH BED REVELATIONS

— 1926

CHAPTER I

"I fall upon the thorns of life; I bleed!"

THIS is the story of a woman's life. The most famous — or notorious — woman in the world, it has been said of me, and I think that is a fitting estimate. One New York newspaper alone maintains in its files eighty-one bulky packages of newspaper clippings that recount the twenty-year tragedy of Florence Evelyn Nesbit and Harry Kendall Thaw. One package of clippings is all they have about Theodore Roosevelt.

Wherever the English language is spoken the name of Evelyn Nesbit Thaw, dragged these two decades through the mire, is a synonym for Magdalene — and woman's woe.

But this is not to be a book of lamentations. Rather is it a record of hope, a story of how the tranquility of triumph came to a woman whose life has been a battle with merciless circumstance, a ceaseless struggle against prejudice, poverty and scandal.

I am telling the whole unvarnished story for the sake of truth and justice, for the sake of my son, whom calumny has hounded as it hounded me. I shall tell everything, frankly and without passion or prejudice, for I hold no hatred in my heart

1

for anybody — not even for the spectral memory that once was Stanford White.

Life is worth living for its drama, even though we are fated to play the parts that are deepest in suffering.

It is all like the shadowy pageant of a dream now, in which I observe myself as a detached personality, moving with other figures of the past down the glittering vista of Broadway — back where the path begins to fade into the first years of the century. Go with me, and I will retrace all those steps as I took them.

I will unlock the secrets of my heart and bare the confidences, through all these years untold. I will answer the questions that have puzzled a curious world.

Why did Harry Thaw kill Stanford White? Was I the sole cause?

No. I was merely the inciting spark. The murder done that tragic June night in Madison Square Garden twenty years ago was the culmination of an old enmity between the millionaire youth and the artistic sybarite. They hated each other long before either of them knew me at all. There were other women — many of them — who might have been the immediate cause of the deed. Fanny Belmont, Edna Goodrich — these were two of the girls who had "cut" Harry Thaw and bestowed their friendship upon his rival, Stanford White. Long before the shooting on the roof garden there had been a flash of weapons between them — White instead of Thaw was the one who drew the revolver that first time. Friends of both felt that one would have killed the other sooner or later, even if I had not been the luckless pawn whom the fingers of fate moved between them.

Was Thaw really insane?

There is much to be said on that subject — much delving to be done in the dark closets where the Thaw family skeletons lurk. The real cause of the first break between us was the stories I heard at the time of that terrible trial, when I went to Harry in jail and asked him if they were true. I do not know. I am no psychiatrist, no alienist, and my opinion would be worth nothing. All I know is that Harry Thaw can be an awfully sweet and loving man — and he can be the antithesis of such a man.

Did I love Stanford White? Did I love Harry Thaw? Is Russell his child? Did my mother "sell" me as a child to a rich man?

These and many other questions I propose to answer freely and fully — how I became Stanford White's girl; my affair with Thaw, our trip to Europe, our marriage, my confession to him; behind the scenes in London, New York and Pittsburgh society; my life with Jack Clifford; my attempts to win success and my failure.

My story is the story of New York in the first quarter of our century, a story of shifting hues and sound and fury, of light and shade, of silver clouds with a dun and sorrowful lining.

Many are the changes that have come to Broadway with the passing of the old order. I came upon the scene in the days of hansom cabs and "seagoing" hacks; of long hair, long dresses and the "Florodora" sextette; of Nan Patterson and "Diamond Jim" Brady in his comparative youth. The motion picture and the phonograph were infant toys, the automobile a dubious experiment.

I was fifteen when chance threw me into the vortex of New York. That was in 1901. Pittsburgh was my birthplace, just as it was Harry Thaw's. My father was a lawyer, a man of intelligence and fine integrity, but, unhappily for me, he died when I was a child. After his death my mother removed to Allegheny City, Pa., where for a time she conducted a boarding house.

Later, we went to Philadelphia to live, and it was there, through the interest of a friend, that I got my first work as an artist's model. I posed for a number of painters — they were all head studies, for the artists were interested primarily in the childish beauty of my face. We were getting along fairly well in Philadelphia, but modeling was poor pay and jobs were very infrequent, so I urged my mother to let me try bigger fields. What I wanted to do most was to go on the stage, for I realized there was very little future in simply posing for occasional artists at so much per hour.

My mother was steadfastly opposed to my stage ambitions, but she consented to take me to New York. I was confident I could make a stage connection, one way or another. My Philadelphia friends helped by giving me letters of introduction to a number of New York artists, among them Carol Beckwith, and I started out on the path that was to lead me to my paradise — and then back down the other side of the hill of fame to ashes and remorse.

The New York artists were very kind to me, and very much interested in me, and did much to help me along. They described my beauty as something that had nothing to do with lines or specific features, but as a universal and *diffused* sort of beauty. I hope no one will try to read any element of conceit into such references. My youth and my costly beauty are so far behind me now that I speak of such things as one detached and impersonal and almost disinterested.

At any rate, the New York newspapers began publishing full-page "layouts" of my photographs and the pictures painted of me. I was hailed as a new and unusual type of American beauty. Prince Henry of Battenberg, it seemed, had selected a rather ordinary-looking St. Louis woman as the one he considered "America's most beautiful girl," and one New York newspaper published a page of my pictures with one of the other woman and the query:

"If Prince Henry thinks this is America's most beautiful girl, what would he think of Florence Evelyn Nesbit?"

That was before I had gone on the stage, before I had met Harry Thaw or Stanford White, so I may be forgiven for mildly boasting that not all — not quite all — the billions of words of publicity I have received were due entirely to that terrible tragedy.

This more or less flattering recognition of my beauty helped me greatly. A mere slip of a girl of fifteen, I started out on a stage career the very first year I was in New York.

Ted Marx, a theatrical agent, saw a head that Carol Beckwith had done of me, which was reproduced in a Sunday supplement. He sent me a note, in which he styled me "the girl with the Madonna face" and invited me to get in touch with him if I thought I would be interested in a stage career.

Bubbling with happiness and anticipation, I fairly floated on the way home to our tiny, tawdry little flat in Twenty-second Street, west of Seventh Avenue. I waited until after dinner to tell my mother of the offer. She was outraged; she would not listen to me. She insisted it was out of the question. That night I thought of a plan to overcome the difficulty.

Mother had always argued with me that theatrical men were all villains, wolves in sheeps' clothing and the like. I knew from the tone of Mr. Marx's letter that he could not be any of these things that mother had read about in fiction and adopted as her conceptions. I wrote to Mr. Marx, asking him to call on us Sunday afternoon. That, indeed, was when my mother was always in her best mood.

Ted Marx called. Mother was furious, but Ted was a clever talker. He evidently knew how to handle people, particularly women. Before he had been at our house an hour mother had invited him to tea. Before he left that evening he had given me my first contract. And that was the way I broke into Broadway. I landed in the world-famous "Florodora" company, then in the midst of its original long run at the Casino Theatre.

The stage was very new to me, but very fascinating. Perhaps the one thing that made me appear the amateur I was to the girls whose dressing room I shared was the way I put on my make-up. I had used cosmetics, of course, while posing as a model, but this sort of make-up was not appropriate for the strong footlights of the stage. It was Frances Belmont herself, the woman over whom Stanford White and Harry Thaw had almost come to blows before I knew either of the men, who taught me how to make up for the stage. I learned quickly how to apply the paint and powder myself and before long I felt as if I had been in the spotlight for years.

Edna Goodrich's mother had been playing with Anna Held. She left the French star's company and came over to "Florodora," in which she played a minor part, and Edna Goodrich was in the company as well.

When mother came to call for me after the evening

performance, as she did every night, she met Edna Goodrich's mother and they became fast friends. She told my mother that she had changed from Anna Held's show and taken the small part in "Florodora" primarily in order to be on hand to see that no harm came to Edna. My mother thought it an excellent idea, and every night the two would discourse on the wicked ways of Broadway and the guiding influence of mothers so necessary to young girls on the stage. At the time Edna and I thought it a good joke. Neither of us dreamed how desperately true were the things they said.

It was Edna's mother who persuaded my mother to permit me to attend my first luncheon party. The invitation was from a man named Stanford White, who, Edna's mother explained, was a celebrated architect and a person popular in the highest ranks of New York society. I think that both our mothers were under the impression that Mr. and Mrs. Stanford White were to entertain me and Edna — that was why mother permitted me to go.

But they were tragically wrong.

CHAPTER II

*"Man's love is of man's life a thing
apart —
'Tis woman's whole existence!"*

STANFORD WHITE was a magnetic man, a fascinating man, a forceful personality. No doubt he was a genius.

Much of his work stands today as monuments to his skill in architecture and design. Of the millions who pass annually beneath the beautiful memorial arch of Washington Square, at the foot of Fifth Avenue, probably very few realize that it was created by Stanford White. The old Madison Square Garden, which he designed and where he met his death, is no more. The Herald Building, said to be the finest example of pure Italian Renaissance architecture in America, still stands on Broadway at Herald Square, though somewhat altered. These and many other magnificent edifices are lasting, solid epitaphs to Stanford White, the artist.

Man's love, as Byron said, is a thing set apart in a man's life, but it is the whole of a woman's existence. Stanford White, the artist, like a great many other people of artistic temperament, believed himself above "petty conventions." He loved me, I am sure, for in a great many ways he proved his affection and consideration. The fact that he also had a wife whom he loved did not keep him from loving me, nor, according to his view of such things, was it essentially wrong, except in so far as it was likely to cause unhappiness to others.

Years and suffering teach us charity and tolerance. If once I was bitter toward Stanford White, I am no longer so. I tell what I have to tell dispassionately and with no thought of reviling the memory of one who has been measured by a higher justice than ours.

I met him, as I related in a previous chapter, at a luncheon party to which Edna Goodrich had invited me, at his behest. It was a party at his Madison Square Tower studio, and in New York's bohemia, as you may know, a chaperone is no more welcome than a battery of adding machines. Chaperones there were none, and the only other invited guest was Reggie Ronalds, a young society man.

Stanford White was a tall, stalwart, robust, handsome man, with reddish hair and the most genial of smiles. From the moment Edna Goodrich presented me to him and he took me by the hand I was fascinated.

He radiated charm. He was full of a vigorous enthusiasm — a sort of Rooseveltian personality with infinite refinements. He was happy in the presence of beautiful things — and beautiful women — and you caught his infectious spirit. It was not surprising that he won the steadfast devotion of many men and women.

After the luncheon we went into a tiny, mirrored room that he had arranged, perhaps to flatter women's vanity, perhaps to multiply the charms of women for the artist's or roue's purpose of appraisal. For Stanford White, you know, was a worker in the graphic arts, as well as an architect, and he occasionally made use of a model.

In his mirrored room I could see myself, at least externally, as others saw me. The four walls, the ceiling and even the floor were paneled with mirrors. It was like multiplying many times the efficiency of one's French three-tiered vanity. I could see every side of myself without moving my head — profile, full face, three-quarters, full length, feet and all. Stanford White stood in the doorway, an amused smile playing about his lips as he watched me studying myself. I had no conceit, only curiosity. I had always wondered what artists thought so beautiful about me.

Edna Goodrich seemed to get uneasy because Stanford White was showing me so much attention. It was she who suggested that we go to the swing room and "have some fun," and we adjourned to a unique retreat upstairs. The first thing that struck you, in contrast to the lavish decorations of the studio, was the absence of furnishings. The main bit of equipment was a swing suspended from the ceiling, made of wound silk cord with a small satin-quilted seat. A huge Japanese umbrella hung near the ceiling, within the radius of the swing, and as Stanford White pushed me toward the heights I saw what the idea was — I kicked my feet through the umbrella and squealed with delight. Pulling a rope on the side wall caused a new place on the umbrella to swing around, so that Edna, too, had much fun kicking new slits into the big Japanese toy.

When Edna was in the swing, with Reggie Ronalds propelling her, our host addressed to me his first personal conversation. I had been holding my handkerchief to my face every now and then because I had a sharp toothache. Not wishing to appear indisposed lest Edna suggest our leaving, I had tried to conceal my distress, but Stanford White had guessed the trouble. He asked me to let him see the "wicked tooth," and then he gave me a card with the name of his own dentist on it, declaring my mother must take me to see him at once.

Of course, we could not afford to pay the fees of a dentist who had millionaires as his patients. My mother angrily sent the card back to him, for she was incensed when she learned that the party was a studio affair and that Mrs. White was not present as hostess. White evidently had hoped my mother would do that very thing. It gave him an excuse to call the following Sunday afternoon to ask her pardon for his seeming presumption.

With his culture, his charm, his poise, Stanford White won my mother over instantly. He appeared to be merely a kindly old gentleman — he was around fifty, but he looked much older — who wanted to do things for people less fortunate than he. Indeed, there is evidence that he was very generous to many people who needed help — art students, poor boys who wanted to study architecture, and many of that kind.

Every Sunday after his first visit to our shabby little three-room flat Stanford White sent a victoria carriage so that my mother and I and my little brother Howard could go riding. Not once did he appear anxious to accompany us.

He engaged me to pose for him, and the famous "Beauty and the Beast" photograph, was made at White's work studio.

There were other studio parties. The second I attended, I believe, was given in honor of Elsie Ferguson. There was nothing particularly noteworthy about the luncheon. I remember the food was sent in from the Manhattan Club, nearby.

Meanwhile the friendship between me and Edna Goodrich seemed to ebb into a kind of indifference. I never knew whether Edna was jealous because Stanford White had made me his protegee or whether she simply lost interest in me. It was my impression that she was rather indifferent toward White.

Just what my own feelings were in relation to Stanford White I scarcely knew or had time to analyze then. I was bewildered with the newness and the glamour of Broadway. I had tasted of the sweets. Success for me seemed sure, for I had won the patronage of distinguished men. I had gained already a sort of fame. My earnings were large enough now to justify our removal from our poor quarters on Twenty-second Street to the Audubon Hotel, at the corner of Broadway and Thirty-ninth Street, near the theatre where I was playing. It sounds preposterous today that we paid for our suite of living room, bedroom and bath in the Audubon the princely sum of $15 a week.

My mother was wearied of New York and the lack of the home touch. She wanted to go back home and call on the old neighborhood friends. She hated New York, not for its coldness, particularly, but for its formality.

I remember telling Stanford White laughingly how old-fashioned my mother was; the idea of being homesick for Pittsburgh, when you could live in New York, the centre of art, of fashion, of letters, of science, of culture — of life! Only too often the centre of despair.

He called the following Sunday afternoon and cleverly manoeuvred the conversation to Pittsburgh and the "old folks at home." My mother talked about it eagerly, but said she could never go back on a visit without taking me, and it wouldn't do to interrupt my work when I was doing so well.

"There's no reason in the world why you shouldn't go and leave Evelyn here," said Stanford White. "I'll keep an eye on the young lady for you."

People have said since that mother should have known better than to let him persuade her. The fact is that no other man I have ever known could have done it except Stanford White. He had the charming and disarming ingenuousness of the artist. There are such people who do wrong, not malevolently, but innocently. They believe themselves "beyond good and evil;" that morality is largely a matter of rules and regulations which are hypocritically obeyed, not for hope of reward, but for fear of punishment. I think that was largely White's philosophy, as he outlined it to me in after years.

My mother did not "sell" me to a rich man. Such talk is cruel falsehood. She did let him pay for her trip back to Pittsburgh, but she trusted Stanford White up to the time of his death, five years after our first meeting, and always regarded him as the one true friend I had to whom she could appeal. She did appeal to him after she and I had quarreled bitterly on the subject of Harry Thaw. She always regarded Thaw as the villain in the plot and Stanford White as the magnanimous hero. I had never told her the truth. I had never told anybody but Harry Thaw — prior to the time I went on the witness stand and gave the last of my poor, tarnished possessions to save the life of the man I loved.

My mother went to Pittsburgh. Stanford White had engaged a drawing-room for her, had ordered flowers for its beautification, had seen that a basket of choice fruit was delivered by a Fifth Avenue fruiterer. Then he accompanied me to the station to see her off.

It did not seem a crisis, that parting. And yet you know that feeling of something gone from your heart, an odd, numb vacancy that comes even with the temporary departure of one who is dear to you, one with whom you have been constantly. Sometimes it seems to have the melancholy touch of death — that feeling of the vacant room.

Not loneliness alone, but something akin to death, waited for me that day when mother left.

Stanford White was kind to me. He took me to dinner that first night, so that I need not dine alone at the hotel.

And one or two nights later he invited me over to his studio for a little dinner party with some of his friends.

We waited, and the friends never came.

"They turned us down," said Stanford White, laughingly. "Well, that's no reason we should go hungry."

"Hadn't I better go?" I asked him.

"Nonsense! Why should you?"

We had dinner, and I drank a glass of champagne. I thought I was a wicked little sinner, doing something perfectly devilish.

Today our hands go up aghast at the younger generation. There have always been and always will be poor little flappers — and "flaming youth."

After dinner I said something about going, and Stanford White reminded me that I hadn't seen all of his establishment. There were several floors of it, and he conducted me about, pointing out the precious art objects which he loved with the devotion of a connoisseur.

At length we came to a room I had never seen before.

The most beautiful bedroom in America.

CHAPTER III

"And down the long and silent street
The dawn, with silver-sandaled feet,
Crept like a frightened girl."

DAYBREAK!

Whether it is gray and bleak or warmed by the rose-glow of returning hope, there is something tragic about the beginning of day.

One of the vividest word-pictures of all literature, to me, is that of the morning when Dickens's hero, Sidney Carton, having spent another night of wine and debauch, went out to meet the dawn and read in its ironic beauty the truth of his failure, his tragedy, his worthlessness to life. It was then he determined, you remember, that if he could be of any use to anybody by giving his poor, spent life, he would have accomplished one good thing in death.

I think, like Carton in "A Tale of Two Cities," I would have died willingly on the guillotine, if it could have done anyone any good, that morning when the accusing dawn crept in the windows of Stanford White's studio bedroom.

Gray morning picked at the velvet curtains and fingered in the shadows things of sodden beauty — for every object in

15

that room, delight as it may have been to artist and connoisseur, cried out to me in shame and ugliness.

I had been crying all night, it seemed.

All I could remember was that I had gone into the hateful, enveloping loveliness of that room when night was there with its soothing cloak of unreality. There had been a bottle of champagne on a table, and Stanford White had urged me to drink some of it. It tasted like all wine to me. It all tasted bitter. But this was the deadliest, cruelest cup of all.

Stanford White tried to comfort me with his cynical philosophy. Nobody was "good." It was all sham and pretense. What anybody did was nobody else's business, as long as it harmed nobody else. It was all in the way you looked at it. Human society was all a senseless maze of rules of conduct impossible to observe. There was no harm done. The real crime lay not in its commission, but in being found out. Expediency ruled the world, said White. We all did, not what we thought was right or wrong, but what we thought would cause least trouble, least inconvenience, least distress.

"Rationalizing" — that's what they call it in the insanity books, of which I have read every one I have been able to put my hands on. The craziest of us can find "sensible" reasons for the most irrational actions — we all do it in more or less degree, but the lunatics go to extremes, presenting very specious proof that they are Richard the Third, Napoleon or Julius Caesar.

So much for philosophy. It's wordy bunk!

A great many clever writers have said I lied when I told my story on the witness stand at Harry Thaw's trial. But where, oh, Mr. Jerome, was my motive for lying? For mercenary reasons? If money had been my object, I could have kept my mouth closed and let Harry Thaw go to the electric chair. I would merely have been a very rich widow. The past of a girl who could not help herself might have stayed buried for all time.

I told the truth and reaped my reward — when I had done all I could for the Thaws they were through with me. "That girl" they cast out as the many, many pure and virtuous people of the kind world have cast me out. I reaped the reward of truth — sneers and rebuffs, ostracism and calumny, a name forever blackened as that of "the most notorious woman in the world."

So much for truth. Perhaps Stanford White was right, and the copybooks wrong.

But let me get back to my narrative.

Stanford White, with all his faults, had a thousand good qualities, and one of them was an innate gentleness and kindliness. He did many things for me, for my mother and my brother, Howard, too, that he need not have done.

He was anxious for me to improve my mind — his friends have said that his interest in me was primarily intellectual, rather than otherwise; that he had found a new medium in which to work, more fascinating than the plastic art — the development of a young girl's mind. Almost every day, he came by the hotel to leave books for me to read. By and by, he said, I must go to school and receive a more thorough educational grounding, if I aspired to do really worth-while things on the stage. And I did — it was a consuming ambition with me.

Very gradually Stanford White built up in me a faith and a sort of blind admiration for his genius, as well as a friendship responsive to his kindly nature. I do not know to this day whether I ever really cared for him. Perhaps there was too great a disparity in our ages. I only know that he held a strange fascination for me, and that I found myself going to him with all my problems.

"Florodora" was about to go on tour, and my mother absolutely forbade me to accompany the troupe. She had come back from Pittsburgh after a happy visit, and found me apparently the same child she had left in Stanford White's care. My mother never knew — until the whole world knew — what had happened in her absence.

It was just at this time, as I recall, because it was near the close of "Florodora's" run, that I met Harry Thaw.

I did not like Harry at once. I found him arrogant, unpleasantly abrupt, undoubtedly spoiled and accustomed to having his own way in everything. I had developed a little temperament myself, by that time, and was not a little spoiled by the attentions that had been paid me by men both rich and famous.

It was at a luncheon at Rector's that I met him. My friend, Elva Kenny, a beautiful Irish girl, who was in "Florodora," had asked me to have lunch with her and another girl, who, as it happened, could not keep the engagement. While Elva and I were chatting, a tall, slender man who looked about thirty, entered the restaurant, caught sight of Elva and came smilingly to our table.

After they had exchanged greetings, she turned to me and said: "Evelyn, you ought to know this man if you're from Pittsburgh. This is Harry Thaw. I want you to meet my friend, Evelyn Nesbit, Harry."

I smiled at him and he glanced toward the empty chair at our table. "May I join you?" he asked, and we assented.

Harry and I did not get on so well at that luncheon. Elva Kenny found our clashing wills a good joke, and told me afterwards how much she had enjoyed the dessert episode.

I wanted to order apple pie for my dessert, a favorite with me to this day. Harry Thaw carefully scanned the menu and told me bluntly that I would have ice cream. He proceeded to order it, in spite of my protests, and needless to say a perfectly good saucer of strawberry ice cream melted away before me.

Years later Harry Thaw told me, when the subject came up again during an argument, that he had a perfectly good reason for ordering ice cream instead of pie. He had determined at that instant that I was going to be "his girl." Therefore, I had to keep my perfect complexion — and pie is bad for the complexion! I mention that trivial episode because it was so typical of Harry Thaw. He had always had what he wanted.

When I told Stanford White about the chance meeting in the restaurant, he was very much disturbed.

"Don't have anything to do with that man, Evelyn," he warned me. "Harry Thaw is insane!"

Two days after our meeting, Harry came to see me. I told my little brother, Howard, to say I was "not in." Our suite was a tiny one, and in order to escape the visitor's notice while Howard answered the doorbell I had hidden in a wardrobe. Just as my brother was preparing to close the door, I lost my balance in my cramped position and came tumbling out on the floor, as startled and frightened as Harry Thaw was angry. He had brought me a bouquet of orchids, and he was so furious with me that he crushed them to bits and dashed the fragments at me through the half-open door as he went stormily away.

My mother was furious with me for having been so rude. Like all mothers, she wanted a "good catch" for her daughter.

Stanford White's attentions to me had begun to arouse her suspicions.

"Surely, child," she admonished, "you are not thinking seriously of a man old enough to be your father, are you? He is a married man, Evelyn — never forget that!"

Meanwhile "Florodora" packed up and went on the road. I left the show in order to remain in New York, and my influential friends did not permit me to remain long without an engagement. My second stage appearance was made in a comic opera called "The Wild Rose," written especially for me and produced by George W. Lederer.

I saw nothing more of Harry Thaw during this time. I was not interested in him, for another man, nearer my own age and profoundly attractive, had come upon my horizon. He was Jack Barrymore. He was not on the stage at this time, but was winning public notice as a cartoonist on the staff of The New York Evening Journal.

Once I mentioned, half jokingly, that I would like to see this budding genius. Stanford White had made it a point to grant my every wish, said he would arrange to have Jack Barrymore meet me at a dinner party.

The party was at White's studio in the Madison Square Garden tower. I liked Jack Barrymore at once. He was such a boy and so clean and wholesome; it was a relief to find some one nearer my own age who could talk to me in the language common to youth.

Stanford White showed his first streak of jealousy that night. Jack had a trick of drawing clever little pictures on his immaculate cuff and holding out his hand to me so I could see them. It disturbed White to find me so easily amused by another man. Jack drew a clock, marked in the hands, and then wrote a date beneath it. I nodded my head. It was Jack Barrymore's unique way of asking me if he could come to see me.

Not long after this party Stanford White's customary program for the year called him to the Canadian woods for a fishing and hunting trip. Jack Barrymore came to see me, on the date we had agreed upon, and then he called again. To be perfectly accurate, he took me to Rector's every night for two weeks.

One evening my mother went to visit a friend in Brooklyn, and I knew she would not be home until late. She had always kept me to the rule of being home early, and there had been no exceptions. But this night the cat was away and at least one mouse felt skittish.

Jack Barrymore and I danced every dance at Rector's. He ordered champagne recklessly, one quart after another. I scarcely felt as though I had had any at all, and was having a perfectly wonderful time dancing, until suddenly it hit me. I found to my amazement that I could not walk steadily back to the table.

Jack offered me some consolation because he was practically in the same state himself. We got into a hansom cab, and Jack managed to tell the driver where he lived. There we went, little caring what the direction was, so long as we were riding — away over to Jack's apartment on the East Side.

There, in Jack's living room, he did some eloquent Shakespearean lines for me, swinging about his shoulders the wide cloak of Romeo his distinguished father, Maurice Barrymore, had used.

And it was there my mother found us. We had "passed out" about as completely as Romeo and Juliet did. I was sound asleep on the couch, and Jack was slumbering dramatically on the hard, unfeeling floor.

I can assure you we caught Hail Columbia. Stanford White returned unexpectedly from Canada and called to see me the next day while my mother was soundly berating me for my misconduct. White seemed stunned. He sent at once for Jack Barrymore, and some hot words passed between them. With all his youthful gallantry, Jack offered to marry me if there were no other way to stop spiteful gossip. Ethel Barrymore heard of it and called, in great excitement, at our hotel to beg my mother not to permit such childish folly.

But I had no intention of accepting such a sacrifice on poor Jack's part. We finally convinced everybody that it was all just a silly lark, and the excitement blew over.

Stanford White was not taking chances, however. He and my mother decided the safest place for me was a boarding school, and without much further ado they packed me off to the DeMille School, at Pompton, N.J.

And it was there the plot did most of its thickening — for Harry Thaw came back upon the scene.

CHAPTER IV

"Is there respite in nepenthe?
Quoth the Raven, 'Nevermore!'"

My memory looks back through the fevered years to a quiet, sedate, tree-shaded haven in New Jersey, far from the maddening clangor of Broadway.

There I was sent for a respite from the whirl of life — from the influences that had dragged me down, and were dragging me deeper. Curiously enough, it was Stanford White, at once malefactor and benefactor, who made the arrangements for my withdrawal from stage and studio and the gay night parties of New York's bohemia.

Mrs. DeMille's school at Pompton, New Jersey, might have been the source of great permanent benefit to me had circumstances — and Harry Thaw — permitted me to remain there.

Stanford White's interest in me, as I have explained, was not a sentiment wholly unworthy. He had come to regard himself as my protector and champion — perhaps his conscience told him he must do everything in his power to atone for the harm he had caused. He felt responsible for my spiritual and mental, as well as my material, well-being. He thought I should not continue to spend my girlhood years in the unhealthy and artificial atmosphere of New York's gay circles. So he sent me to Pompton to prepare myself for better things.

White was not a saint. Neither was he the bestial creature which overheated imaginations pictured him as being at the time of that infamous trial. He was an intellectual, not a person of purely sensual tastes as his enemies declared him to be. He was as keenly interested in the development of my mind as he was in my physical beauty.

I liked Mrs. DeMille's school, but, as intimated in my schoolgirl diary introduced by Mr. Jerome at the trial, my first thought was, "I wonder how far this is from Rector's?" I longed for the stage, but I was quite convinced that if I did not prepare myself for it by proper schooling I could not hope to achieve a genuine and worthy success. I was ambitious, too, in a literary way. Stanford White had told me that I had a splendid mental equipment, that my mind was quick and keen and versatile. And during the short time I had been under his "tutelage," he declared, I had gained a broader knowledge of the English classics than most women twice my age. Samuel Hopkins Adams, one of the exceedingly numerous writers who expressed themselves at the time of the Thaw trial, was kind enough to say my sketchy little school diary showed a striking "clarity, purity and simplicity of style."

I owe much to the DeMille School. The principal tutors under whom I studied were not quite so famous then as they are now, but they were earnest and able young men who knew their subjects thoroughly. They were Cecil B. and William C. DeMille, known the world over today as motion picture directors who nurture the highest ideals of art in their profession. They were the sons of Mrs. H. C. DeMille, who had founded the school at Pompton, and they were giving their arduous efforts to help keep the lovely old place for their mother. English and art, the principal studies in the curriculum, were taught by the brothers, and occasionally other tutors from Paterson would come out to hold classes in special subjects.

FROM HER OWN DIARY

It is no reflection upon one of the DeMille boys — I have forgotten now which one it was — that I called him a "pie-faced mutt" in my diary. Perhaps I was prejudiced against all schoolmasters when I first arrived. My diary put it this way:

> Mrs. DeMille was very nice and said, "Come right in, Evelyn," so I jumped with all the agility of a soubrette and proceeded to go in. When we drove up to the mansion, Mrs. DeMille's son came up smoking a pipe, and I must confess he is simply a pie-faced mutt. That quite describes him.
>
> I was taken into the house and shown to my room. It is neither large nor small, and has Japanese paper on the wall. There is a white bed. So I went to my room and took a nap. The last thing I remember thinking was, "I wonder how far

I am from Rector's!" Rector's, I
know, is really not a proper place
for an innocent young person, but
I always had a weakness for it.

And another passage, of which Mr. Jerome made much
capital at the time of Harry's trial, for in those good,
hypocritical days, such sentiments from a young girl were
enough to condemn her:

When one gets into a regular swing
and does certain things at a certain
time and learns something each time,
one thinks there is lots in life after
all, and a girl who has always been
good and never had a word of scandal breathed about her is fortunate
in more ways than one. These girls
are all like that. They have been
kept from the world all their lives
and know very little of the mean
side of it. And then, on the other
hand, there is not one of them who
will ever be "anything." And by
"anything" I mean just that. They
will perhaps be good wives and
mothers and die good wives and
most people would say, "What could
be better?" But whether it is ambition or foolishness, I want to be a
good actress first. Of course, I

couldn't live here all the time, but I can enjoy it for two years at least.

My schooling would not have been interrupted, the whole future course of my life would have been altered and the world no doubt would have been spared one of its ugliest tragedies but for the stroke of chance which took me away from Pompton. I was stricken suddenly with appendicitis. My mother and Stanford White were notified, doctors examined me and counseled immediate operation, and I was whisked to New York in an ambulance. You may well believe it was not any ruse on my part to get back to Broadway, for the attack was serious, and for days I lay between life and death in a sanitarium in East Thirty-third Street.

HARRY THAW'S HECTIC WOOING

Stanford White had called to see me a number of times at the DeMille School. He had not permitted Jack Barrymore to call, and I was glad of it, for the tempest in a teapot that had developed from a silly lark of ours had almost driven me frantic.

White, meantime, had had no further qualms on the subject of Harry Thaw, for as a matter of fact I had heard little or nothing from the gay and wealthy young Pittsburgher. But Harry learned I was back in town, heard I was sick — he had called my mother casually and inquired about me — and then it seemed he conceived a sudden and overpowering determination to have me for his own.

He came to see me at the sanitarium and preceding his arrival there was delivered to my room a great bouquet of orchids and azaleas. The news that Harry Thaw, of Pittsburgh, was showing attentions to me created more excitement among the hospital attaches than the knowledge that I was a friend of Stanford White. Harry was widely known, quite often in the newspapers, you know, long before he met me. He had been "written up" time and again for indulging in such escapades as only a spoiled and petted son of wealthy parents could afford or "get away with."

At the first college he attended, Wooster University, in Ohio, young Thaw had been known as "the cigarette fiend." He was reprimanded by the president of this respectable institution for such stunts as entertaining the entire chorus of a musical troupe that played at the local theatre, and for inducing all the show girls to wear during the performance bows and garters of black and old gold — the Wooster colors. Urged by the college president to settle down and choose a course of studies that he liked, Thaw replied that he had already selected his major studies — penmanship and lawn tennis. Then he disappeared from school, and the president received a telegram from him, dated New York:

"I'm off to Europe to buy some cigarettes.

"H. K. THAW."

Harry and Wooster University could not get along together much longer, even though the college had been heavily endowed by Harry's mother, and every effort had been made to tame Harry down. He tried a university in the East, and for some reason or other was "shipped" again. Harry said it was for playing poker.

At the close of his college career, Harry settled down to follow the giddy profession of just a rich man's son. Harry's father, a self-made man, who had risen from the bottom of the metal trades to the position of a multimillionaire, had stipulated in his will that Harry should be cut off with an allowance of $200 a month as his share of the family's forty millions, until such time as Harry should show "discretion and fitness" to handle money. His mother, however, was not so stern with him, and raised his allowance to $80,000 a year, which is enough to keep any young man in cigarettes, even at this day.

Both in Pittsburgh and New York, preferably in the latter, Harry achieved a fame — of sorts. A Sunday supplement described him as "one of the four wildest young men in New York." In a fit of subtle humor one night he decided he wanted to walk through a plate-glass window in the Imperial Hotel. This he accomplished, somehow, without gashing any arteries, and, as he paid cheerfully for the damage done, the affair was successfully smoothed over. On another occasion, when he had reached a captious stage of intoxication, he wandered into a resort known as the Garrick, attacked a negro porter who displeased him and made reasonably good progress toward wrecking the place. He was hustled into Yorkville Court, where he professed a willingness to pay for the damage. Next he broke up a performance at Weber & Fields' Music Hall, thrashing several attendants and breaking up as many fragile things as he could lay his hands upon. It was a dull month when some misdemeanor of his did not break into the news. Sometimes it would be a thrashed cab-man, sometimes an attempt to ride a horse up the steps and through the door of an exclusive club, the loss of $40,000 at poker, or wrecking of all the glassware on the Hoffman House bar, at a cost of $300. A lively time was had by all whenever Harry was on the scene.

Of course, I did not know about all this when I first met

Thaw. Most of the things had happened before I came to New York, and all I knew was that Harry had a reputation as a rich man's son who did much splurging and spending. He did not confine his activities to America, either, I was to learn later. In Paris he proceeded to repeat his New York and Pittsburgh performances on a larger and more glittering scale. His debut in the French capital was marked by a "beauty dinner," which, at a reputed cost of $50,000, he gave in honor of a bevy of gay Parisian ladies at the Cafe Coucou.

$1,000 FOR ONE BAND

This banquet gave Harry the European status he craved. He followed it with another at a hundred dollars a plate, and with an entertainment at which Sousa's whole band furnished the music, the bill for the latter item alone being $1,000. He was now a central figure in Paris. He had "arrived." One of the noblemen he met was the young Earl of Yarmouth, who later came to America and married Thaw's sister, Alice.

It was early in 1902, at the zenith of his career as spendthrift, hail-fellow and eccentric good-timer, that Harry's erstwhile wandering fancies seemed to concentrate on one definite object — Evelyn Nesbit, the famous artist's model, "girl with the Madonna face" and protegee of Stanford White.

When Harry called to see me at the sanitarium I was not long in learning that his interest in me had become intensely sentimental.

The attentions of a millionaire who was an acknowledged "catch" among the Broadway showgirls should have flattered me to a degree. Perhaps they did, but I was not thrilled by Harry's words as another girl in my place might have been.

When Stanford White came to call that evening he had

heard, through a nurse, of Harry Thaw's visit. Needless to say, he was very angry about it.

"Evelyn," he scolded me, "didn't I tell you to keep away from Harry Thaw? The man is a demented ne'er-do-well. I'll not have him hanging around here!"

"I kept away the best I could," I said, with a weak sort of smile. "It wasn't I who did the visiting."

There is more truth than rhetoric in the homely adage, "Every knock's a boost" — especially where a young girl's love affairs are concerned. Many parents have learned that the best method to throw a daughter into the arms of a suitor whom mother and father despise, is to constantly "run him down," and forbid the girl to see him.

Criticism of this kind on the part of my mother and Stanford White directed at Harry was responsible more than anything else for the fact that I fell in love with Thaw, ran away to Europe with him, married him — and went as far as any woman can go for a man, quite farther than the merciful gates of death, when I went on the rack for the master inquisitor, Jerome.

Thaw and Stanford White had quarreled over women before, as I mentioned in a previous chapter of this series of articles. Fanny Belmont, of the "Florodora" company, with which I found my first theatrical opening, had been a "flame" of Harry's, and following a bitter misunderstanding they had been reconciled. Presumably everything was patched up, and, to prove that it was Harry who had made the first overtures of peace, Fanny boasted that she would make him give a supper party for everybody in the cast.

Harry consented willingly. He went immediately to Sherry's and made preparations for a lavish after-theatre entertainment which, even for those days, cost a small fortune.

After the show, Fanny Belmont ordered hansom cabs for all. She got into the first one and directed the drivers of the other cabs to follow. And instead of going to Sherry's, she led the way to Stanford White's studio!

Harry Thaw sat alone up at Sherry's until after midnight, waiting for his guests. He had engaged two orchestras and a sumptuous ballroom for dancing. The musicians grew restless, but Harry, determined nobody could make a fool of him, ordered them to play for him alone.

THAW AND WHITE NEAR BLOWS

Raging with anger when he realized he had been made a dupe, Harry went to Fanny Belmont's apartment, and there, possibly because she had been instructed to do so, Fanny's maid told him where her mistress could be located. In a terrible blaze of emotion, Harry went to Stanford White's studio, nearly bowled over one of the girls who opened the door at his insistent pounding, and turned the torrent of his wrath upon White, rather than Fanny Belmont, who was the cause of it all. Girls who were present at that party told me Thaw and White almost came to blows. Stanford White leered at the enraged youth and nonchalantly invited him to have a cigarette. Harry dashed the gold case from White's hand, and, without a word to Fanny Belmont, rushed from the apartment.

Harry Thaw had always been under the impression, and, perhaps, justly so, that it was a sort of sport with Stanford White to see how quickly and gently he could wean away any girl who had bestowed friendship upon Harry. The same thing happened, I was told, in the case of two of the most prominent actresses on Broadway, both of whom were said to have "turned down" Harry in favor of White. It was rumored one time, that in his own defense White had pulled a revolver on Harry.

Such was the basis for the enmity that existed between the two men long before I came on the scene. I was to be the unlucky spark that would ignite the powder magazine of Thaw's hate for the architect.

CHAPTER V

*"Thus conscience doth make cowards of
us all."*

SHOULD a woman tell all?

Should she confess everything to the man who loves her?

Sometimes I think the things we consider the bravest are the most cowardly, and deeds that the world calls craven are the most courageous. And quite as often our acts of so-called virtuous sacrifice, of self-effacing martyrdom, are only the weakling's way of surrendering to stress.

It would have been a far braver, far more righteous thing, if I had left my secrets dead in the cemetery of my heart.

But I told Harry Thaw, and from that moment of egotistical shriving sprang all the ugly hours of horror and sadness and tragedy that have been built into a nightmare of twenty years for us both.

Thaw and I were in Paris.

An attack of appendicitis and the necessity for an immediate operation had caused my removal from the girl's boarding school at Pompton, N.J., where Stanford White and my mother had sent me. And it was at the New York sanitarium where I was taken that Harry Thaw came back into my life.

White knew that Thaw had been to see me at the hospital, but he did not know that Harry, in his headlong, impulsive way, was plotting to steal me away from him.

When I had recovered sufficient strength to go back home, I found Harry Thaw had persuaded my mother that she ought to take me to Europe, so that I could have a long rest, with nothing to worry about, and a chance to recuperate. Harry told my mother he wanted to marry me — that he was going to marry me, and nothing in the world could come between us. He was so vehement about it that mother was afraid to cross him. He arranged for our transportation and payment of all our expenses, without giving my mother a chance to protest. And inasmuch as Stanford White had made the self-same suggestion, it seemed to my mother the safest thing, to avoid trouble all around, would be to accept Harry's proffer.

Thus it was that we went to Europe in 1902, with Stanford White's consent and approval, and my mother, knowing of the enmity between the two men and bearing in mind what White had said about Thaw, did not tell White that Harry had figured in our plans. My mother was sorely beset, poor woman, and scarcely knew which way to turn. Circumstances had woven for us an already tangled skein of intrigue — there seemed no turning back.

I was a child, a foolish child, and moreover, weakened by illness. I couldn't help myself, and I simply let other people do my thinking for me.

As far back as I could remember, I had longed to go to Europe, and every other consideration was pale and meaningless compared to the prospect of this adventure.

Packing for the trip was an absorbing delight. I did not know then that one carried little wardrobe to Paris. Pilgrims bound for the gay capital usually go with their trunks quite stripped of their finery. The trip back from Paris brings those empty trunks packed to capacity with the newest creations for which the fashion center of the Western World is celebrated. But mother and I, inexperienced voyagers that we were, labored for days getting our things ready and packed so they would not wrinkle. We sailed on the American in May, 1902.

Harry Thaw had said that he would see us in Paris. He had planned to pay his yearly visits to friends in various parts of Europe and then to wind up his trip in Paris, where he promised to join us and show us the sights.

Mother selected a small apartment on the Avenue Matignon, just off the Rond Point. It was typically French, with the small balconies outside long paneled windows. Inside everything was painted in odd colors, and there was an abundance of silk draperies and old lace. The apartment was beautifully decorated, but it lacked, like so many of the finest European places, the modern comforts of American hotels and apartments.

Harry Thaw kept his promise and joined us, presently, in Paris. He was more generous, kind and gentle than he ever was before or afterward. I was still weak from the effects of my illness, and it was Harry himself who would carry me upstairs to the apartment when we came in from a sightseeing trip that had been a little too much for my strength.

My mother, meantime, had become restive. Her attitude toward Paris was disappointing to me, for I had expected her to be far more excited over the pleasure city of the world than I was, since she had spent most of her life in a small

Pennsylvania town. Not long afterward I discovered the real cause of her dissatisfaction was Harry Thaw's redoubled interest in me.

Every morning Harry would phone me from his hotel, and consult us as to our wishes and plans for the day. He did everything possible to make things pleasant for me and my mother, but mother had grown to dislike and distrust him. Stanford White had written her, and probably had told her still worse things about Harry. She urged me to write to White, though I did not want to. She insisted that I should not appear ungrateful for his many seeming kindnesses to us, and so I did write him several letters.

The friction that had been developing between my mother and me on the subject of Harry Thaw kindled into flame when we left Paris and went to London. There it was we had our first — and last — bitter quarrel. She told me she would rather see me dead than to sacrifice myself for a man like Harry Thaw. It was her strong conviction that Harry was a dissolute young villain, and that Stanford White was a kindly old gentleman who was merely taking a fatherly interest in me and trying to save us both from pain.

I had begun to feel that Harry Thaw really had been wrongfully abused. His attitude toward me had been merely one of respectful adoration, and I liked him more because of the criticism that had been heaped on him. My mother announced her determination of going home, and begged me to go back with her to New York — and Stanford White. This I refused to do, and in the heat of our quarrel I resolved to cast my lot definitely with Harry Thaw. I wanted to see Europe, and I was willing to break with my mother to stay on and enjoy life.

Harry Thaw and I toured Europe. We went to Switzerland, and there Harry was arrested for speeding in his automobile. He told the authorities I was his wife, and the news traveled back to America many times faster than Harry's car had gone. Harry had begged me to marry him, because the last thing he was desirous of doing was to injure or compromise me. I had steadfastly refused, and perhaps he thought that by boldly announcing the supposed fact he would influence me to do as he wished. But for Harry's sake I did not want to marry him. I knew sooner or later the gossip about Stanford White and me would become public property, and would reach Harry's ears. I was sure Harry's marriage to a showgirl and artist's model would appear "disgraceful" to his family, and that it would bring only sorrow and distress to him.

We went back to Paris, and he took me to the "Cafe au Rat Mort" and a few of the other so-called "underworld" places that are maintained chiefly to shock and amuse tourists. There were no "orgies," anything of that sort. Harry took care to avoid the seamy side of things Parisian.

Soon, however, he began to reveal the less lovely aspect of his disposition. He was stubborn and domineering, and demanded his own way in all things, even to the merest detail. Once when we were about to go for a ride, I came downstairs in a white Summer frock and blue picture hat. Harry, who was waiting for me in the lobby of the hotel, demanded that I change my hat and put on a small one. I explained that I had worn the broad-brimmed hat to protect my face from the sun, but he was obdurate. To avoid a scene, I went to my room and changed hats.

It was a trifling detail, but from that time forth Harry was a veritable martinet. Not long afterward there was a similar occurrence, and we had some bitter words. It was the first real quarrel that we had had, and it was serious enough in its consequences to cause a break in our friendship.

I went back to New York. I sailed with Elsie DeWolfe and Elizabeth Marbury, whom I had chanced to meet in Paris. Back on Broadway, the three of us put up at the Savoy Hotel.

I got a part in a new production, "The Girl from Dixie," which, ironically enough, opened at the Madison Square Theatre. Its prospects looked good, but unfortunately it lasted a very short time after the opening night. I was out of a job again — and out of funds.

Simultaneously with the closing of the show, which had been some weeks in rehearsal, Harry Thaw came back to America. He was repentant and asked forgiveness for his conduct. Again he begged me to marry him, and it was clear that the short period of our separation had only served to intensify his determination. He begged me to go back to Europe with him, vowed that his only wish was to protect and care for me always.

Again I sailed for Europe, with Harry Thaw.

We visited some places where we had not gone before, and for a time we lived in a superb old castle on the Rhine that Harry had rented, a base from which we took motoring trips to many points of interest.

It was one June night in Paris when the crisis in our lives was reached. There had been another of our perennial discussions on the same old subject — marriage. I had used every argument that I could think of — I had told him every one of my reasons but the real one. I told him it would be an advantageous thing for me to have the protection of his name, but an unfortunate thing for him. I told him everybody in New York theatrical circles knew about me and Stanford White, and it would be unfair to him to have people linking the name of his wife — his name — with scandal.

He demanded to know why I felt so unhappy because of the friendship of Stanford White, and I told him why I could not marry him — I told him everything.

I thought it the just thing to do, but the moment the words left my lips I knew I had made a terrible mistake.

Harry Thaw's face looked suddenly blanched and thin. Even his lips went bloodless, and there was a look of horror in his eyes that grew into a glare of rage.

He paced the floor, moaning like a wounded thing: "Oh, my God, my God! If only I had known you — if only I could have saved you!"

I am convinced that if Harry Thaw was ever mentally unbalanced, it was caused by the revelation I made to him that night in Paris. Hatred of Stanford White became an obsession with him, and at the same time his love for me grew into something of worship. He exalted me far beyond my deserts. He grew to regard me as an angel of purity who had been cruelly wronged.

CHAPTER VI

". . . . Nor all our piety or wit
Can coax it back to cancel half
a line,
Nor all our tears wash out one word
of it."

I HAD told him!

I had made the mistake which so many women have made in the long, sad annals of their sex.

"Mistake," you say, "to tell the truth? Is not the truth worth any sacrifice? Have we not been taught all our lives that to tell the truth is to shame the devil?"

Yes, we have been taught that. But the relation of man and woman is essentially one of untruth. It is bound up in man's idea that woman is his property, and must do as he says, but not as he does. And man, who himself created the double moral code providing that what is wrong for a woman is not wrong for a man, knows perfectly well that there is no truth or justice in that code. Always he will continue to browbeat his women with the threat of that medieval law, with the shame of "consequences," with the fear of disgrace — always serene himself in the knowledge of his own immunity.

41

He knows in his heart that his attitude toward women is hypocritical and merciless. Yet he weaves a romance about her, with threads from his threadbare double code. He is prone to exalt her in the name of chastity, for purposes of his own self-illusionment. Occasionally he must work himself into a fury of egocentric self-pity, and kill the woman who has flouted his double code, or kill himself — or kill the man who has done no more than he himself would have done, and felt no qualms about it.

Enmeshed in such a relationship, should a woman tell everything?

If she wants to be a martyr — yes! If she gets any pleasure out of self-flagellation — if she wants to wreck her life, her husband's life, and destroy perhaps the permanent happiness of others — yes!

If I had never told Harry Thaw about Stanford White, I would be nearer today what might be called a "happy woman." I should have escaped these years of terror that only the huntsman's quarry can know. I should not have been on the rack for the sake of the thing that men call purity.

Harry Thaw never recovered from the shock of what I told him in Paris.

Often afterward I would awaken to hear him moaning in his sleep, or he would rouse me from a sound slumber and question me interminably about Stanford White, would make me rehearse in every sordid detail what I had told him. I think he never got it out of his mind until Stanford White was dead. He had dedicated his life to two things — punishment of White and provision for my happiness.

He was not resentful toward me because of my confession, and far from convincing him that he ought not to marry me, what I had told him made him doubly assiduous in his pleading.

When we went to London on the way home, he openly registered at a leading hotel as "Harry K. Thaw and wife." It was his way of forcing the issue, and he defied Stanford White, his family and all the rest of the world to stop him.

In London, we had another bit of a tiff because of a silly prank of mine in attending the Countess of Yarmouth's ball without an invitation. The Countess was Harry's sister Alice, who, learning that Harry was in town, had urged him to come. Harry had not wanted me to attend because I might be a target for gossip. As it happened, I came upon a showgirl friend whom I had known in New York called Billie, who had been engaged to dance at the ball in a professional capacity. Billie through error had received a formal invitation, and I borrowed it from her.

Imagine Harry's amazement when, as he was chatting in his best Sunday manner with a lady of nobility, I came face to face with him. Much to my surprise, he neither ignored me nor flew into a rage. He merely bowed stiffly and continued chatting with his peeress.

He scolded me later for having done a very indiscreet thing, but he did not lose his temper. We were scarcely happy, though, as we made our way to the steamer, and the passage to New York was fogged in an aura of gloom.

We were besieged by reporters on our arrival home, all clamoring to know whether we were married or whether we were not. Harry and I left the pier separately, with the understanding that I was to join him later at the Hotel Cumberland. There Harry refused to register us as man and wife, or to register at all, and the manager politely refused our patronage.

Harry went to Pittsburgh, and I went to stay with a friend at the Gregorian.

It seemed there was only one course left for me now — to yield to Harry's protestations and become his wife.

Worry over the situation and the unenviable publicity it had brought me had left me on the verge of a breakdown. My first operation for appendicitis had not proved entirely successful, and I had suffered because of it from time to time. Now I had a severe case of nerves to make matters worse, and I found myself back in the sanitarium.

Harry tried in every way to make up to me for the suffering he had caused me, but he was suffering acutely himself. His curious, disjointed, irrelevant letters indicated the mental stress which he was enduring. If I had known at the time they might be manifestations of the dreadful "paranoia" of which I was to hear so much two years later, I might have been able to help overcome it.

It was a belief of Harry's — a delusion, if you like — that Stanford White had hypnotized me. Once when we were driving in Paris, he had stopped to go into a hypnotist's booth, though he did not tell me why.

Now I was getting letters from him like this:

"I've something very important to tell you. When I first saw you when we were together, I saw clear through even then, and you meant absolutely right; you were hypnotized, I think, but you meant no wrong. You know I never lie to you. I have thought very carefully and I promise you I will never hurt you at all.

"I didn't mind you having my letters. You know now every word was true. Shall I tell you something? You have in 3 weeks gotten a reputation as dangerous. Also for telling scandals false or true. (SEALED SECRET.) Take back your Elba. How would you like what you did at Lincoln, without asking, retold. Only I understand and therefore respect you the same Angel.

"Also they say you are going to pieces and in 8 months will be in the gutter, morally and mentally and dishonorably. You can't materially for me.

"Your mother must trust her friend who spoiled your birthright as a lady and made your father's name a byword and hers and will always make Howard's.

"She knows this well. Ask her. She will say she knows I was respectful and modest always. If you had only let me save you before you were 16. It would never be known.

"I am trying to forget, but when I reached our home then sat at breakfast with the decentest people in the world, and not dull. Oh, you should have been there. Twice I had to leave the table so they could not see . . ."

I think he must have been drinking when he wrote such letters to me, which accounted for their rambling and sketchy character. But I was to hear from the lips of Harry's mother how cruelly he was suffering.

She came to see me after I had left the sanitarium and was living on Madison Avenue. She begged me to marry her boy, for she said it was the only thing that would save him. She told me how he often left the dinner table in tears, because he could no longer stand the strain under which he was suffering. She told me how she found him staying up until the small hours of the morning, staring moodily out of his window, or moaning to himself.

"I admit I am selfish," said Harry's mother, "but I am going to ask you to care for my boy. He needs you. If you will consent to be Harry's wife, I shall do everything in this world to make you happy."

I was sorry for Harry Thaw. I felt responsible, very largely, for his unhappiness. And I had nothing but respect and admiration for this worthy and kindly woman who was his mother, who had put aside her pride to come to me on his behalf.

I consented to marry him, and a week later when Harry joined his mother in New York, all of us talked it over together in detail. A month afterward, Harry and I went to Pittsburgh and were married. My mother gave her consent to the match and was present at the ceremony.

There followed our honeymoon tour through the States, principally the Pacific Coast, and a somewhat extensive camping trip in California. I was sorry when it was time to go back to Pennsylvania, for I was not eager to take up the duties of the conventional "young matron of society."

There was an intensive course of training in store for me at Lyndhurst, the beautiful but austere mansion of the Thaws. The most eminent and expensive tutors were engaged to teach me foreign languages, music and all the social graces. It was really an eight-hour day for me — union hours — and while I realized it was something I very much needed, still I felt somewhat as I had felt when Stanford White and my mother sent me out to that girls' boarding school at Pompton, New Jersey. This being a millionaire's wife was hard work.

It had its compensations, of course. Society everywhere gave me the utmost respect. I was the lawful wife of Harry Thaw. The past had been obliterated by the stroke of a pen and the wearing of a wedding ring. Everywhere, the most representative families were only too eager to invite me to their luncheons, their teas, their whist parties.

But there were constant bickerings among the Thaws. It was most uncomfortable to live with them, as indeed it is for most newly married couples who take up their residence with "in-laws."

The Fall and Winter of that year I lived at Lyndhurst. There were many petty disagreements between Harry's mother and me. The servants, shopping accounts and carriages were at my disposal — technically — but whenever I attempted to use these privileges there was an aftermath of heated argument and hysterical unpleasantness. Once, I remember, I was in Pittsburgh shopping for some Winter clothes, when I wandered through an antique shop where an auction was in progress. I purchased a small marble bust of Diana, and because I had the thing sent out in my name instead of Mother Thaw's name, there ensued the most disagreeable dispute imaginable.

With the constant flare-ups over what seemed to me unimportant trifles, I was almost a nervous wreck. Harry always took my part during the innumerable tilts, and this made matters worse, because his mother resented it.

We stood it almost a year, and I was unutterably relieved when Harry made a suggestion that we make our plans to go abroad again, early in the Summer of 1906, and to stay there as long as we liked.

Thus it came about that we went to New York in May of that black year, en route to Paris. We never sailed, for reasons known to all the world.

The fact of our marriage had not erased the shadow of Stanford White.

CHAPTER VII

*"The hands of the sisters Death
and night incessantly, softly wash,
again and again, this soiled world."*

THE reputed wickedness of Stanford White was an
obsession with Harry Thaw.

He had a Stanford White "complex," at first suppressed
in his brain, but growing all the more in virulence as the years
passed. For three years he nursed a hatred for the man — and
three years from the month when I confessed to Harry that
White had bewitched me, Thaw shot him down.

During all that time he never made a reference to White
without calling him "the blackguard," which he spelled in his
letters as it is pronounced, "blaggard."

White made efforts to win me away from Harry before
we were married, though not afterward. When I returned from
Europe after my first trip there with Harry and my mother —
and after I had quarreled with my mother — White did
everything in his power to make me break with Thaw. Much
of it was done at the request of my mother, who constantly
wrote to White and begged him to "save" me from Harry Thaw.
To the very end — the climax, I should say — my mother

innocently regarded White as a benevolent rich man who had befriended us simply because he took an interest in my aspirations toward an artistic career. I don't think she was ever convinced to the contrary.

Thaw looked upon himself as the consecrated avenger of the wrongs, real and fancied, that Stanford White had committed. He constantly talked of "putting that blackguard behind the bars," and he did try, several times, to have Stanford White arrested and prosecuted. At one time he went to Anthony Comstock, famous as the then president of the New York Society for the Suppression of Vice, and demanded that he take action against White. He complained bitterly because Comstock would not take notice of his charges. As a matter of fact, I suppose there was little or no real evidence available.

In April, 1905, fourteen months before the killing of White, Harry added a codicil to his will, under which he bequeathed the sum of $17,500 to various persons named, "to be used in obtaining legal redress and substantial damages from one————and one Stanford White, of New York, N.Y., and for the benefit of one————, upon whom a degrading assault was committed in the Spring or Summer of 1901, by the said————and the said Stanford White, who, accompanied by an older woman, induced the said ————to enter the house about————Street, New York (a house furnished and used for orgies by several inhuman scoundrels, as was well known to many persons in New York) under false pretenses of ordinary social conversation. And then he administered sedatives or cocaine, or by other means did render the said————in a semi-comatose condition."

Harry's will named several young actresses then on the stage in New York as the supposed victims of White, and provided that money should be available "to obtain legal redress and substantial damages for some other American girl victim of the said Stanford White's treacherous assaults." Among the men to be entrusted with the expenditure of the bequest for this purpose were Anthony Comstock, Frederick W. Longfellow, Harry's attorney; Adolph Marks, of Chicago, and "Richard Roe" Berry, of Washington. It was provided that "should the said Stanford White not survive me three months after the probating of my will, all bequests in this codicil become void."

Harry's strange will was presented at the trial as a bit of evidence of Harry's alleged insanity. Certainly it was a manifest that his ruling passion was a desire for White's punishment.

I was at first fearful of trouble between the two men, though I never imagined it would be any more serious than a fist fight. Harry's animosity and his threats had continued over such a long period of time that they had lost, to me, much of their force. You know the old adage about the barking dog never biting. I thought Harry's hatred had spent itself in words and there would never be any serious consequences.

It is not true that Stanford White pursued or annoyed me after my marriage to Harry Thaw. He did, as I have said previously, attempt to alienate me from Thaw before we were married. When I returned from Europe after my first disagreement with Harry, Stanford White told me I must go to the office of Abraham Hummel, who, he said, was "the second biggest lawyer in New York." Hummel, in my presence, dictated an affidavit in which some of the wildest and most idiotic charges were made against Harry Thaw, regarding the supposed way in which he had treated me in Paris. It accused him of beating and maltreating me dreadfully, and of all sorts of other wild conduct.

I refused to sign it, in spite of Hummel's bulldozing and his leering intimations that I might fare handsomely if I started a breach of promise suit against the young Pittsburgh millionaire.

Some time later I signed some sort of paper in Stanford White's office, foolishly not stopping to read it, and later I learned it was the self-same affidavit. I made it so hot for Hummel and White because of this trickery that, in my presence, they burned the affidavit in a jardiniere in Hummel's office — not, however, until after they had made a photograph of it. This photograph was used as evidence against me at Harry's trial. It was evidence enough, I think, of the unsuccessful efforts made by White and Hummel to use me as an instrument in injuring Harry Thaw.

After my marriage to Thaw, they left me alone, but Harry was still both jealous and fearful of White. He may have heard rumors, which he did not care to repeat to me, concerning White's supposed efforts to continue annoying me. Suffice it to say that when Harry and I went to New York, in the latter part of May, 1906, on the way to Paris, Harry still bore his old enmity toward White.

The spirit that in earlier days had found an outlet in bizarre pranks and childish mischief was souring now into a revengeful, quarrelsome sullenness. I think he suspected every casual admirer of sinister designs on me. Without my knowledge, at the time, he employed private detectives to shadow Stanford White and "get something" on him. White knew of it, and it worried him. He told his friends about it, and they advised him to hire detectives to keep him in touch with what Harry was doing. I think the principal thing the Thaw and White detectives did was to watch each other.

One day we encountered Stanford White on Fifth Avenue, when our carriage and White's chanced to meet, White rose in his seat and waved at me, calling "Hello, Evelyn!" and that was enough to cause Harry to fly into a senseless rage. He made me promise him solemnly that I would tell him about it every time I saw Stanford White thereafter, even if it were only on the street. He said if I didn't tell him he would find out about it some other way, and there would be "trouble, sure enough."

The time neared for our departure to Europe. On the evening of June 25, 1906, Harry invited two friends to join us at a little farewell dinner at Martin's, following which we were to go to Madison Square Garden and see the opening performance of a musical extravaganza called "Mam'zelle Champagne."

I saw Stanford White at Martin's. He had been there for dinner with his son, Lawrence, and a college chum of the latter, and I caught a glimpse of him just before he left. He bowed to me and smiled.

Had it not been for the fact that one of our companions had seen him, too, I would have said nothing to Harry about it. But knowing his ungovernable temper and fearing he would learn of the fact later and jealously accuse me of trying to suppress something, I wrote Harry a note on a slip of paper and passed it to him:

"The B-G was here a moment ago and went out."

"B-G" was Harry's abbreviation for blackguard.

If he was agitated at the time he did not show it. He merely nodded and crumpled the piece of paper in his hand. If he knew himself that Stanford White had been there, as was later reported, and heard Stanford White make any remarks derogatory to me, neither I nor our friends knew anything about it. The story told later was that Harry had overheard him referring to me sneeringly as "common property."

We went on to Madison Square Garden after dinner, and none of us, I think, had the least idea that Stanford White would be there, too. That was merely a fateful coincidence.

We were in our seats when the curtain went up for "Mam'zelle Champagne." I observed that Harry was not particularly interested in the play, but that was not unusual for a man of his nervous temperament. During the intermission he excused himself and began walking about the aisles restlessly.

I did not see Stanford White when he came to the roof garden at about nine-thirty. After taking leave of his son and the latter's friend, who were going to another theatre, White had dropped in at the Manhattan Club for a chat with friends, and later had come to Madison Square Garden to see the last act of the new Summer play.

Toward the end of the play, Harry again asked us to excuse him. I was watching the play and did not notice that Harry put on his dark gray topcoat. A number of people were leaving the Garden, and there was slight confusion.

Stanford White was sitting at a table near the southern end of the Garden and was idly watching the play alone, his friends having left him for the moment. The first hint I had of approaching disaster was the sight of Harry threading his way through the tables to the southern end. Then I saw Stanford

White, and every muscle in my body seemed to fail me. There was a burlesque dual scene in progress on the stage, and as from a great distance I heard the words of one of the actors:

"Let the dual go on!"

Almost at that instant there were three sharp, deliberate reports of a pistol.

The architect had looked up to meet Thaw's glare, but he did not make the slightest effort at self-defense. Thaw had whipped out a revolver and fired three shots into his victim's breast.

White staggered from the table and crumpled to the floor.

Harry lifted his weapon, "broke" it to empty it of its cartridges, as if to reassure the witnesses of the terrible deed they had nothing to fear, and started calmly toward the exit to the elevator.

It had all been so sudden, so free of the turmoil and angry voices that usually accompany such scenes, that hundreds of people in the Garden did not know what had happened. Many thought the shots had been fired backstage, and were a part of the "business" of the play.

A fireman who had been detailed to the theatre stopped Harry and took the pistol away from him as he neared the elevator. Thaw made no resistance.

"He ruined my wife," said Harry, almost coolly, as a policeman hurried up.

I rushed to the elevator as they were about to take him down and threw my arms around his neck, sobbing:

"Oh, Harry! Why did you do it?" was all I could cry, over and over.

Harry tried to quiet me. He was strangely composed himself.

He handed the policeman a ten-dollar bill. "Here, officer," he said, "telephone to George Carnegie. Tell him I'm in trouble."

Then they took him away.

The shot had been fired that was to reverberate many times around the earth — that was to echo and re-echo the name of Evelyn Nesbit as "the most notorious woman in the world."

I was so shocked, so dazed, that I did not even remember the name of the hotel where I was staying. One of my companions took me downstairs and hailed a hansom cab. He knew my hotel was the Lorraine, but he would not let me go there. He told me every newspaper reporter in New York City would be there clamoring to interview me, and would make the night more hideous for me. He urged me to tell him the name of some friend with whom I could stay and who could be trusted to keep the secret of my presence, at least for a few merciful days.

I thought of May Mackenzie. She it was whom Stanford White had told — so Harry Thaw believed — that some day he would "get Evelyn back."

He would not get me back now — ever.

He was dead. Oh, numb and horrible death!

CHAPTER VIII

"She did not need to do it . . . . But,
for no other purpose than to save this
ungainly and unnatural Thaw, she laid
upon the altar the last sacrifice of
womanhood, and accepted without a
murmur, dishonor and shame for the
years before her."
—John Temple Graves.

SELF-PITY is a grievous fault, and I have fought against it. I don't think I have ever been sorry for myself, and if I appear somewhat in the role of martyr in this story, it is merely because the facts speak for themselves, and there is no other way to tell it.

Harry Thaw was my husband, and I loved him. He had killed a man who had wronged me. For my sake he had placed his own life in danger. It seemed only natural and just that I should stand by him when he needed me.

Nobody had to ask me to do what I did for Harry's sake. At the first conference of the Thaw attorneys, after Mrs. Thaw had hurried back from Europe upon receipt of the dreadful news of her son's plight, I was called in and questioned. I told them all I knew, and I offered to go on the stand and repeat every word of it if it would do Harry any good.

The Thaws raised no objection to my contemplated sacrifice. The hero of a story book would have gone proudly to the electric chair, rather than permit his wife, the woman he loved, to disgrace herself in aiding him; but I encountered none of this heroic quality among the Thaws. As a matter of fact, they were terribly distressed and upset, and scarcely knew what they were doing. The first set of attorneys retained for Harry insisted the only hope lay in a plea of insanity, but this Harry stormily refused to permit. He declared he was not insane, and that he was not afraid to take his chances of an acquittal on the grounds that there had been extreme provocation for his act. In spite of his mother's pleading, he demanded a change of lawyers. The "unwritten law" and temporary or "emotional" sanity were substituted.

Those were terrible days of anguish and anxiety for all of us in the early Winter of 1907, when the first trial was in progress. The verdict of those twelve men in the jury box would, I was told, probably depend upon my own testimony — Harry Thaw's life, in other words, was in my hands.

Our lawyers did not deceive me concerning the nature of the ordeal that awaited me. They told me that a skillful and merciless prosecutor, one of the ablest men in his profession, would trick and trip me, bulldoze and harass me, would do everything in his power to discredit me. I was to learn that they had warned me truthfully. If anything, they understated the diabolical cleverness of William Travers Jerome.

I went into court that first morning with all the sensations of one already condemned, yet with firm resolve to hold back nothing, to tell everything I had come to tell.

Harry's eyes met mine as I took my place on the witness stand, and he smiled encouragingly. I knew that the first part of my testimony would be drawn from me by friendly counsel, but my story was one that no woman could tell with complacency. In many respects I found this first day the worst of all, more trying, indeed, than the cross-examination which followed.

I described the various parties I attended in White's studios, the things he did to befriend me, and finally the events of that fateful week when my mother went to Pittsburgh and left me in New York.

"What did you tell Thaw concerning the things that happened after your mother left?" the lawyer asked me.

"I told him that Mr. White sent me a note inviting me to a theatre and supper party. I told him that Stanford White had arranged for a carriage to come for me every night at 7 o'clock to take me to the theatre, and to meet me after the show and bring me home. I told him that this carriage was waiting for me. When I got to Stanford White's place he was there alone. There was no one else there. I asked him where the others were. He said, 'Oh, they have turned me down; they did not come.' I was very much disappointed that we could not have the party, but he said, 'That's all right, we'll have it anyhow.' He said he would show me over the house, that there were some rooms I had not seen. He took me through all the apartments. The walls were covered with mirrors and had something on them that looked like green glass, and there were stained glass windows. I could see my own reflection in the mirrors. On the next floor there was another sort of studio. There were paintings on the walls and sofas all about. There was a secret stairway in the back of this room and beyond that a bedroom. We went to this room and sat down. In the back of the room was a large picture. He told me about it. In the room there was some wine — a bottle of wine on the table. Stanford White poured out the wine and gave it to me. I told Stanford White that I did not want to drink the wine. He came over and asked me why. I told him I did not care for it, but I finally tasted a little of it. It was very bitter and I put the glass down.

"Then I felt a thumping in my head and I began to get dizzy and I felt my senses slipping away. Then I became unconscious and remembered nothing more. I told Harry that I woke up several hours later in this room."

At this point I broke down and could go no further. The judge made a gesture at the lawyer as though he should not question me any more. Harry took out his handkerchief and hid his face and sobbed aloud. It was several minutes before I could go on.

"Then what did you do?" asked the lawyer.

"I screamed and screamed. He got up and gave me a kimono and told me to put it on. I dressed and Stanford White took me home in a carriage. I don't think he spoke to me. He brought me to my room. I sat in a chair all morning. Next day he came around to take me to dinner again. I told Harry that Stanford White came into the room, knelt down on the floor and kissed the hem of my dress. I would not speak to him at first.

"I told Harry what he said to me. He told me I must not be frightened or worried at what had happened and asked me to look at him. He said that he had not hurt me, but that he thought a great deal of me. He said that I must not be worried. He said it was necessary to send mother away and that I must not tell her anything about it. He said that I must never tell anyone about it. I told Mr. Thaw that Mr. White told me I was going to have a fine time.

"He said to me that everyone did these things. He laughed and said, 'Yes, they do.' The people I mentioned were people in the show. He said I could go to the theatre and watch them and I would find out that they did these things. My mother was gone a week. Several days later he came to me and took me in an automobile downtown."

When Jerome took me in hand for cross-examination, he dwelt persistently on every tiny detail of my testimony. He tried in devious ways to trap me into a contradiction. There was one point on which he hoped to shake me from my calm. That was the question of money which from time to time Mr. White paid whenever I was out of an engagement.

Jerome pressed me unrelentingly as to all that had happened. There was no evading him. He asked me questions which made me hot and cold. All the experiences of my previous hours under fire were of no avail. There came a question . . . . . . I broke down and wept.

After my cross-examination the members of the Thaw family made a great fuss over me in the witness room and later at the hotel. I was "brave little Evelyn," and "dear little Evelyn," and "most courageous girl," and "wonderful, bless her heart."

How different things were to be when the two long, weary, ghastly Thaw trials were over — and "brave little Evelyn" was of no further use!

The newspapers referred to me in very kindly terms during the first trial, and I am sure public sympathy was on my side and Harry's, but I had spoken the words that were to label me irrevocably as "the most notorious woman in the world." The courtroom was crowded beyond capacity every day by people who came hoping to catch a sight of my face. Crowds lined the sidewalks at the Tombs prison entrance, waiting patiently for my daily visit to Harry. They even blocked the doors of the Hotel Lorraine, where I continued to stay. Everywhere I went I was recognized, for the newspapers published page after page of my pictures.

I had no privacy except when I locked myself in my hotel room. I had no escape from the racking torment which the long days of waiting caused me. I was in court every morning, but my afternoons were free, and I wanted to go back to work as a model, in order that I might have something to divert my mind. This Mother Thaw sternly forbade.

The disagreement of the jury at the first trial was a blow to us all, and yet it was comforting — it made us feel that Harry was no longer in danger of his life. If one jury could not agree, it was quite unlikely that another jury would ever convict. Harry had expected a complete and instant acquittal, however, and he was crestfallen when the mistrial was declared.

The second trial, as everyone knows, resulted in an acquittal, but one with a distressing modification — "not guilty by reason of insanity." The fate his attorneys had desperately fought against had overtaken him. He was committed to the asylum for the criminal insane at Matteawan. Indefinite confinement in a madhouse was to be his punishment.

Of course there was a hope of getting him out eventually. If his sanity could be proved to the satisfaction of a jury. He was entitled to periodical hearings, about once a year, and the Thaw millions were not used sparingly in the employment of lawyers, alienists and physicians. But always there was the shadow of Thaw's nemesis — William Travers Jerome. Like the detective in "Les Miserables" who devoted a lifetime to the pursuit of Jean Valjean, Jerome seemed to have consecrated himself to the task of hounding Harry Thaw. Even after his term as District Attorney had expired, Jerome obtained an appointment as special State prosecutor, in order that he might continue to fight the efforts of Thaw to gain his freedom.

Meanwhile a house had been provided for me in Park Avenue, and it was about this time that Mother broached the subject of finances to me. She wanted a definite agreement whereby I was to receive an allowance of $1,000 a month for my support — not a great deal, when you consider the scale of living to which Harry and I had been accustomed.

The agreement was made, but the Thaw family NEVER PAID ME ONE CENT! Checks were issued, and then the bank was ordered to stop payment on them. Various excuses were given me as to the "technical difficulties" of releasing such and such portions of Harry Thaw's income. I was led to believe that Harry's commitment to the asylum had raised numerous legal difficulties. The fact is, I think, that Harry Thaw, egotistical and self-centered as usual, wanted me to continue absolutely and directly dependent upon his personal bounty. He paid my rent, but little else for my maintenance. He was jealous — he was afraid if I had "too much money" I would have too good a time, while he was incarcerated.

Harry had many special privileges at Matteawan, and the favors accorded him there were magnified by his enemies until the thing eventually resulted in a political scandal. I visited him numerous times at the hospital, and during the periods when habeas corpus proceedings were in progress, he was virtually free. At such time he was permitted to occupy Sheriff Bob Chandler's artistic apartment in Poughkeepsie, and there, too, I visited him and we talked over our future as I thought it was going to be.

My allowance from the Thaws eventually dwindled to seventy-five dollars a week, which was paid to me, curiously enough, not through the Thaw attorneys, but through the family physician in New York. The sum was scarcely a fraction of the money necessary to keep up the Park Avenue establishment. I told Mrs. Thaw this, and she said she was sorry; it could not be helped. I sold the beautiful paintings that decorated the walls; I sold my Persian rugs, my jewels, my clothes, in turn. Then I gave up the house altogether and moved to a tiny studio apartment in Thirty-third Street, just back of the Waldorf.

I had picked up the rudiments of sculpture from artists for whom I had posed, and I began to devote myself to modeling small figures. I not only wanted to augment the pitiful income now granted me from the Thaw millions, but I was determined to build a career of my own.

Harry Thaw laughed when I told him of my ambitions. He said I would never amount to anything, except with his aid. I asked him timidly if he didn't think he could send me to Paris, where I could devote serious study to sculpture, and where I could live even more cheaply than I lived in New York, if only he would pay my passage. He derided the very thought. I must continue to be nothing but Harry Thaw's chattel.

Thus the gratitude of the Thaws, with their forty millions, toward "that girl" who had nothing else to give, but had torn out her heart for them.

CHAPTER IX

"Oh, feet that I've held in my hands,
Oh, hands at my heart to catch!
How will you know the way to go,
How will you lift the latch?"

I COME now in my story to the happiest years of my life
— and the darkest years.

There is some recompense for all our sorrow and despair.
If, indeed, happiness is only the absence of pain, as someone
has said, we know how to put an accurate measure upon our
happiness only if we have suffered much.

When my little boy Russell came into my life nothing
else mattered. The ingratitude of the Thaws, the lurking
disgrace of the Thaw trials, the persecution to which I
submitted at the hands of those who seem to think it their duty
to defame the unfortunate, even the constant struggle for the
means of livelihood — these were mere shoddy trifles now. I
saw life from a new perspective, I learned to banish false
valuations. I came to realize the hollowness of "high life."

Far from being crestfallen because the Thaws repudiated
my son, it really caused me gratification. It was exactly what
I wanted, because it meant that Russell was mine and mine

alone.

Mothers who have gone through the ordeal of separation and divorce and bickerings over the possession of a child know what I mean. Others cannot know.

I went to Matteawan to see Harry. He abused me, insulted me, threatened me — he would not give me a chance to tell him my secret. He declared he "would have to kill me" when he got out of the asylum.

Do you wonder that I did not tell him — that I did not care whether he ever knew or not?

I went to Europe, unknown to Harry or the Thaw family physician. They knew I was going away, but they thought I was merely taking a long vacation somewhere in Canada.

I was not entirely forsaken. I had friends. One of them loaned me money for my trip to Europe. Another, Lillian Spencer, went with me. I decided to go to a quiet place in Germany. And so, for almost a year, I dropped out of sight. Lillian Spencer and I engaged passage on one of the biggest boats sailing out of New York, for we felt there would be safety in numbers. As an added precaution to keep from being found out, I completely changed my appearance. When I went on the steamer I was the most perfect middle-aged New England schoolmarm you ever saw. I dressed in an old linen duster, made up my face with paint so that I seemed mildly wrinkled, brushed my hair back to a slick tightness and covered the impossible makeup with the dowdiest hat I could find, surmounted by a motor veil. In my hand I carried an old-fashioned cotton umbrella.

Lillian Spencer was not so well known to reporters. She went down to the steamer — it was the Kaiser Wilhelm der Grosse — and got aboard without being asked a single question. When I arrived in a cab I glanced about me and saw a veritable host of reporters whom I must pass as I went up the companion-way. Many of them I knew — one of them was a chap who had sat in the courtroom throughout both of the Thaw trials. I held my breath, stooped my shoulders a little more, clutched my faded umbrella a little more tightly and trudged on by, unrecognized.

Not until we reached Germany did I venture to get rid of my disguise. Even then I doffed my borrowed garments only a piece at a time, and not until we reached Bad Harzburg, a little town in the Harz Mountains, some two hundred miles from Berlin, did I again resemble Evelyn Nesbit Thaw.

My stay in Germany during that Winter and Summer of 1910 was a tranquil interlude in my troubled career. A tremendous spiritual change took place in me; things that had seemed prosaic before began to develop an infinite sweetness. It was so good to be alive and happy and free at last from unpleasantness. It was like taking a deep breath of mountain air after being confined in a dungeon.

A hotel-sanitarium at Bad Harzburg afforded me every comfort. There was an exquisite marble swimming pool, tinted shell-pink, where I could take my morning dip. Shade trees about the wide building and long white gravel walks that led down to the dells of wood violets and daisies were a fascinating invitation to stroll. Every appointment of the place was provided with a view to its patrons' comfort and composure.

Lillian Spencer remained with me until October, when she was forced to return to America to accept a theatrical contract which she could not afford to forgo. I went to Berlin and entered the "Privat Klinic." The day I stepped from the train I came upon a theatrical manager I had known in New York. His eyes fairly bulged when he saw me. I knew he was wondering if I could possibly be Evelyn Nesbit. I pretended not to recognize him. And it was years later when I met him again on Broadway that he told me he knew who I was when he saw me that day in Berlin. It was all right then, for the world knew of my baby Russell.

My child was born on October 25, 1910, and two weeks later I astonished my nurse and my doctors by announcing that I was going to sail for home. My visit in Germany had been one of idyllic happiness, but I was seized by an intense longing to get back to my friends. Two days after the date I had set I left Germany and journeyed to England, by way of Holland. I found I had overestimated my strength, however, so in London I engaged a quaint old house in the suburbs and stayed there for several weeks. Then I booked passage for America, returning on a steamer bound for Nova Scotia. "Mrs. Jones and son," as we were styled on the passenger list, were not recognized or molested on the way back to New York.

I engaged a little place uptown, in One Hundred and Twelfth Street, far from the bohemians of the theatrical district, and for weeks I lived there, thoroughly hidden. Scores of my old friends passing in automobiles must have seen me wheeling my baby carriage along Riverside Drive, as was my daily custom, but no one recognized me until one day I came face to face with a man I had known when I was a showgirl. I pretended not to recognize him, but he was curious enough to follow me. It was he who gave away my secret.

All day long I was besieged by reporters. By 10 o'clock at night my doorbell was simply worn to a frazzle, and I gave up. I decided to see the newspaper men, announced the presence of my baby and have the thing over.

The following day I had a visit from Harry Thaw's attorney. Harry had seen the newspapers and had wired his lawyer, who immediately came to me demanding an explanation. I told him why I had kept my secret from Harry, and he shook his head gravely. He told me I had made a grievous mistake.

The call of the lawyer was only an empty formality, however, for Harry had already issued a signed statement from Matteawan declaring that we had been separated for five years and that Russell was not his son. It was of a piece with his former declaration to a lawyer of mine that he "didn't give a —— whether she starved or what became of her."

The repudiation did not surprise me or upset me. I was glad to be left alone. I was glad the Thaws did not pounce upon me with their lawyers and their millions and try to take my baby from me.

Thaw peremptorily cut off my small income, and I was left with ten dollars in my pocketbook, a baby to nurse and no way of earning money. The funds I had borrowed were exhausted, my benefactor had died.

Alma Hayne, a showgirl whom I had once befriended with a small loan, came to my assistance and let me have enough money to tide me over until I could find employment.

I got a job in an ice-skating rink, teaching beginners. It was a poor position, at small pay, but I could not keep even it. I slipped on the ice one day and injured my knee. I found myself out of a job, with a doctor's bill to pay.

I moved to smaller quarters as the weeks went by and little money came in. I took a small studio and tried my hand at sculpture again, but art is long, very long indeed, to those who are in need. I failed. My friends helped me from week to week, but I could not sell the figures I modeled.

It was a struggle, but I got through somehow until the Spring of 1913. It seemed my only hope of earning a livelihood was to return to the stage.

I had almost given it up as a bad job when a Canadian friend of mine, who chanced to be in New York for a visit, made it possible for me to meet Albert de Courville, a London producer, who had been "scouting" on this side. With him were Martin Beck and F. B. Marinelli, the international booking agent.

De Courville knew of my work, and it was he who suggested to Marinelli that they find me a partner and put me in a dancing act.

It was agreed. I was to go abroad at once for European bookings. The new eccentric ballroom dances — the Turkey Trot, the Bunny Hug and other predecessors of the Charleston — were gaining a tremendous vogue, and it was my idea to interpret them in solo and duo dancing on the stage.

At Marinelli's office in Paris I met the man who turned out to be a partner in more ways than one. It was Jack Clifford, whom I afterwards married. He was looking for a dancing partner then, and Marinelli was seeking one for me. "Jack," as he was known in Paris theatrical circles, is in private life Virgil James Montani, son of Brigadier-General Joseph Montani, of the Italian Army.

At the London Hippodrome I made my appearance with Jack Clifford in our novelty dancing act. I was billed under an assumed name, for I wanted to make good on my own merits, and not by capitalizing the notoriety of the Thaw-White case.

Our act was a hit. There was no doubt of that either in

our minds or our managers.

Meanwhile, almost on the eve of my first triumph in London, I learned that Harry Thaw had begun divorce proceedings against me in Pittsburgh. I did not care. Let him have his divorce. I would not fight it. Harry, of course, was still in Matteawan, and about this time was plotting the sensational escape that brought him a year's freedom.

When Jack Clifford and I arrived in New York in July, 1913, for our dancing engagement there I was served with papers brought in a suit to collect bills totaling $3,746 that Harry Thaw had refused to pay five years earlier. A millionaire, it seemed, could get away with almost anything.

At Hammerstein's Victoria, where Jack and I were to dance, they billed me as "Evelyn Nesbit Thaw," but I made them take down the posters and change them to "Evelyn Nesbit." I was through with the name of Thaw.

Following a successful engagement in New York, Jack Clifford and I went on the road with our special vaudeville company. At a theatre in Richmond, Virginia, one afternoon I was suddenly and inexplicably arrested. I found the charge against me read, "for appearing at a public theatre, outraging public decency, as a detriment to public morals and a common nuisance to all the citizens of the commonwealth."

It was not our dancing act, for that was merely harmless acrobatics. It was I, Evelyn Nesbit, who was outraging public morals by seeking to earn a little honest money!

The charge, of course, was dismissed. It was merely a vicious gesture of the holier-than-thous. But it had its intended effect. The news spread to every town in which we were to appear. Mrs. Grundy was waiting for us at the railroad station. Women's clubs held indignation meetings.

Sometimes their verdict on the appearance of the "wicked woman" at the local theatre resulted either in a canceled engagement or an empty theatre. In Kansas City, Missouri, a minister of the gospel denounced me, forbidding any member of his congregation to go to the theatre where I was dancing. And so it went. Humanity closed its last door against the woman who had erred, and Charity, pursing its thin and righteous lips, threw stones at her.

Meanwhile Harry Thaw, escaping by means of fraud and conspiracy from an asylum for the criminal insane, had fled to Canada and had become a public hero.

The same people who voiced their sympathy for him as a harried and persecuted champion of the cause of right and virtue, spat upon the wife and child turned out to starve.

CHAPTER X

"Under the bludgeonings of chance
My head is bloody but unbowed."

A **GREAT** many people have wondered why Harry Thaw ever escaped from Matteawan. He could have done it years before he did, for he was allowed the freedom of the grounds and no excessive vigilance was practiced at the asylum. In fact some of his friends had advised him to escape and take his chances of fighting extradition from another State. He was repeatedly told that the combination against him was so strong he would never be released by process of law. But Harry always refuse to attempt escape, declaring he wanted to be declared sane by a jury in New York State.

He made his sensational getaway during August, 1913, about the time I was putting forth a seemingly successful effort to "come back" on the stage. I may be wrong, but I fancy that very fact was what prompted Harry to bolt from Matteawan. I suppose he felt it was unfair that I should be getting so much publicity while he remained in obscurity.

I think it was almost funny that William Travers Jerome chased up to Canada after him, and I KNOW it was funny when Harry's self-appointed, official Nemesis got arrested for

74

playing poker in a little town across the border.

Harry got out of the asylum with the aid of confederates. Once outside the walls, it was only a matter of a few minutes to speed over to Litchfield, Connecticut, in an automobile. But Harry did not stop there, though he had been advised that, once out of New York and in another State, he could fight extradition indefinitely. He kept on to Canada instead, and was immediately placed under arrest in the first Canadian town where he stopped. He had been recognized by a New Hampshire deputy sheriff while a passenger on a train just crossing the border. The deputy, seeing Harry's picture in a newspaper he was reading, as well as an announcement of the reward offered for Harry, followed in an automobile when Harry and his two companions got off the train in Coaticook, Quebec.

Upon complaint of the New Hampshire officer, a Canadian constable placed Harry under arrest on this astonishing charge: "That Harry Thaw was legally convicted and confined for life and unlawfully escaped from the penitentiary."

If the people of Coaticook and Sherbrooke, where he was taken later, were friendly to Harry, the authorities certainly were not. They held onto Harry while William Travers Jerome made hasty preparations to hit the trail in pursuit. Jerome, having secured a commission as deputy attorney-general of the State of New York, sped to Canada on a special train. His own arrest on a charge of card-playing against the peace and dignity of the Dominion of Canada upset his plans, however, and before he could take the necessary steps to gain possession of the famous prisoner he had so long chaperoned, Harry had already been deported. In spite of a writ from the

King's Bench ordering Harry to be produced for a habeas corpus hearing at Montreal, the immigration authorities grabbed Harry out of jail and rushed him across the border. Then they told him he was "free."

But the States of Vermont and New Hampshire were swarming with eagle-eyed deputy sheriffs who wanted to capture the celebrated fugitive. Within a few hours after he had been deported to Norton Mills, Vermont, and had fled across the state line into New Hampshire, he was arrested near the town of Colebrook. Here his detention was based on the fact that a warrant had been issued against him in Dutchess County, New York, charging him and those who aided in his escape from Matteawan with the crime of conspiracy.

After his forcible ejection from Canada Harry's flight was personally conducted by a group of newspaper men who were following in an automobile. "Take me to the New Hampshire line," Harry begged them. "Jerome has the State officials of Vermont 'fixed.' In New Hampshire I believe I will have a fighting chance against extradition."

A place was made for Harry in the car and it dashed East over a winding road at the very edge of the boundary. Talking spasmodically of tickets to Detroit, writs of habeas corpus and his lawyers, Harry urged the chauffeur to greater speed. He wanted to get out of Vermont at all costs. All the luggage Harry had was a box of cigars and he hung on to them for dear life.

They say Harry was very much relieved when the sheriff of Coos County, New Hampshire, took him into custody. He had been a prisoner so long that he didn't know what to do with his liberty. Harry shook the Sheriff's hand cordially and, with no word of protest or reproach, climbed into the Sheriff's automobile. Under his arm Harry still bore his box of cigars.

"Give me a square deal, Sheriff," he requested. "They did me dirt in Canada."

Harry asked the names of the best lawyers in Colebrook and hired them. Then he was taken to a hotel for dinner and afterwards was permitted to undergo a much-needed shave in the hotel barber shop, while the whole population of Colebrook peered through the window and watched every stroke of the razor.

For the next week or so, crowds poured into Colebrook as if there had been a circus in town. Harry settled down for a long siege of litigation. He leased a comfortable house and for more than a year enjoyed life in New Hampshire, while the legal dispute over his extradition went through all the State courts and finally to the United States Supreme Court. He lost on the final appeal, and, in January, 1915, one year and four months after his deportation from Canada, he was taken back to the Tombs in New York, held on a charge of conspiracy.

Harry was tried with four others on the conspiracy charge during March of 1915, and in July won another jury trial to determine whether or not he was insane. The jury pronounced him sane, and for the first time since Stanford White's death, nine years before, he was a free man. It was estimated at that time that the many Thaw trials had cost the Thaw family $950,000, and that the taxpayers of New York had paid $418,615 for the privilege of prosecuting him. **A total of $1,368,000 thus had been spent on the famous Thaw case.**

Harry was free in more ways than one. He was no longer my husband. I had not contested the suit for divorce filed against me in Pittsburgh. I had had enough of courts and lawyers — I knew too much about the power of the Thaw millions. I knew I had no chance to win, and I didn't care if only the Thaws would let me and my baby alone.

Jack Clifford and I tried a second season on tour with our dancing act, but the "righteous element" of the population held so strong a prejudice against "that woman" that continued success was denied me. My manager began to shake his head. Jack Clifford was discouraged, and he couldn't be blamed for it.

The barriers were up against Evelyn Nesbit. The constant public denunciation I received wrecked our subsequent marriage just as it wrecked my chances of earning a livelihood on the stage. The unkind words, the ceaseless gossip that reached the ears of my husband galled him. He couldn't stand the strain of being the husband of "the most notorious woman in the world." We separated.

The public didn't understand. People thought Evelyn Nesbit had gone back on the stage merely to make capital of the long-continued Thaw-White notoriety. They didn't realize that I had waited seven years before trying the stage again, as a last resort, when all other means of supporting myself and my child seemed futile.

Beaten again, I went back to the struggle.

During the year I spent in Germany I had learned something about cooking. I don't remember just how the inspiration came to me, but it was an inspiration — my tea room.

I would open a tea room in the kindest city in the world, so often falsely called the harshest city in the world. New York is kind because it will let you keep your sorrows to yourself. It is too big and too busy to hound you out and lash you with the tongue of slander.

And, besides, it is the home and headquarters of the biggest-hearted people in the world — the improvident, spendthrift, generous, tolerant people of the stage.

The venture was a success. For months my tea room was the rendezvous of my theatrical friends. Every day it was packed to capacity with those good fellows of Broadway who wanted to help out a friend in need, even if they did have to spend their last "two bits" for a sandwich they didn't want. And if they didn't have money they came to pat me on the back, and I think of them now with a lump in my throat and tears in my eyes. They were friends.

And then, when I had begun to climb ahead financially, when I had been able to pay off some of the debts I had incurred, misfortune laid its hand on me again. My safe was robbed. Thieves took four hundred dollars one night after I had closed up the place and gone wearily up the stairs to my bed.

It was a discouraging blow. The margin of profit is small and expenses are heavy in any sort of restaurant venture, and the money I had lost was money badly needed. And then, as though to belie the adage that lightning never strikes twice in the same place, my safe was robbed in the same mysterious manner two weeks later. This time the thieves got seven hundred dollars.

I never really recovered from that crushing loss. It badly crippled my little business that had begun to thrive so promisingly. I had to go further into debt. I tried desperately to hold on, hoping something would happen to turn the tide of my ill fortune. And then one morning the marshal came and moved my things into the street because I was overdue with my rent.

Dispossessed — the shop was gone. It, too, had gone the way of all dreams. I didn't have a place to move my poor possessions — or the money to pay for their removal.

HARRY'S OWN HIGH LIGHTS ON THE THAW CASE.

As Set Forth in the Unexpurgated Edition of His Recently Published Book, "The Traitor."

He First Meets Evelyn — "I knew she was in the chorus, for she came out of the stage door of the Casino. . . I found that her name was Evelyn Nesbit."

The Warning — "But I had heard of Stanford White, and I told her she should keep away from him."

The Proposal — "She knew by that time that she loved me, and I asked her to marry me."

Her Confession — "Hour after hour she unfolded what had befallen her. I tried again and again to find some possible excuse for him . . . . He was a ravisher."

She Accepts Thaw — "Evelyn's resistance to my proposals to marry her continued to be firm. That she yielded was largely due to my mother."

Just Before the Shooting — "We had tickets at a premiere at the Madison Square Roof Garden."

The Slaying — "Half rising, White gazed at me malignantly. I shot him twelve feet away. He dropped."

After the Arrest — "Evelyn was in terrible dread for me, yet she herself was safe at last. *We could have children then.*"

———————

For the first time in my life, I lost my nerve. Always there had been something, before, to give me courage for the fight, but now it seemed the forces of the unseen, too, had leagued with my enemies to beat me down. I was ill, weary — utterly crushed. A sense of the ultimate futility of everything overwhelmed me. What was the use?

I knew I was beaten, and I tried to kill myself.

By a miracle, I was saved. For what, I did not know. My mother had taken my little son to her home to care for him during my illness. He alone was worth living for, I thought, and yet I wondered whether he would not be better off, after all, if I were gone — if I were only a memory, even though a bad one.

I lay there wearily thinking out my problem, and there was no solution. If the world owed a living to its "most notorious woman," I did not know how to collect it. There was not one tiny ray of light in all the gloom and despair that covered me.

And then, as had always happened in the midst of my

deepest trouble before, help came miraculously. Again it was a few folk of the stage who were thinking of me, trying to help me win. And, devious as always in their ways of doing good, they came at me indirectly. They told the editor of "Variety," the theatrical newspaper, that Evelyn Nesbit was in dire straits. And, hearing thus of my plight, Jack Lait, the famous short story writer and newspaper editor, asked me if I would authorize the publication of my memoirs, for a substantial and salutary consideration.

Literally, it saved my life. It brought me new hope, new courage, immediate help.

Jack Lait had once confessed to me that I had inspired one of his show girl characters in his famous series of Broadway stories. He thought I was wonderful "copy," and that my story would have the compelling punch of reality and sincerity.

And here it is, my story.

(THE END)

—AUGUST 7, 1926.

EPILOGUE

— 1924 AND 1926

EPILOGUE

"EVELYN NESBIT GOING INTO YIDDISH PLAY"

VARIETY, June 18, 1924. — Evelyn Nesbit will be the star of a Yiddish play.

She has been rehearsing her singing numbers nightly, and her studies in imitation and pronunciation are said to indicate a remarkable accuracy for one who is not Jewish and who has never lived among the Jews.

Miss Nesbit will open at the Arch Street theatre, Philadelphia, in "Tanz von Todt" ("The Dance of Death"), and will portray a Jewish girl working as a cabaret singer. The booking was arranged by Burns and Smollens, owners of the Arch Street, who have made preparation for her doubling in the theatre and her Atlantic City cafe, the Palais Royal, nightly, using trains when possible and automobiles when necessary, to "cover" the 60 miles. Evelyn will sing two songs, "Yusel" ("Joe") and "Yukele" ("The Hick").

Miss Nesbit's popularity at the Palais Royal is said to be one of the principal reasons for closing the Silver Slipper, upstairs, where Evan Burrows Fontaine, a rival of Evelyn's for front page publicity, had been entertaining as hostess. The Silver Slipper closed Saturday night.

*   *   *   *

"EVELYN THAW BACK ON BEACH; TALKS OF SUICIDE EFFORTS"

Drank Champagne, Then Poison, "If You Know What I Mean," She Says.

ATLANTIC CITY, N. J., Jan. 22, 1926. — Evelyn Nesbit Thaw arrived in Atlantic City yesterday after her unsuccessful attempt at suicide in a Chicago hotel.

And this is what she has to say:

"I had been on the water wagon for six months. I had not tasted liquor of any kind for so long I hardly knew what it tasted like. I had champagne on that New Year's Eve party and it went to my head."

The former wife of Harry K. Thaw smiled a knowing smile. She continued:

"When I arrived at my hotel I started reading a book of essays on 'Suicide.' I just went in the bathroom and drank the poison. I knew what I was doing, then again I didn't, if you know what I mean."

To tell the truth the interviewer didn't know.

Evelyn denied that her nose had been broken at the New Year's party. It only bled a bit, she said.

"Will you ever go back to Harry?" Evelyn was asked. She retorted:

"Say, what do you think I want — a living death?"

Evelyn will again take up cabaret work along the Boardwalk, she declared.

*   *   *   *

April 15, 1924. Photograph of Evelyn Nesbit on
the beach at Atlantic City, N.J., with her dogs.

DANCES OF TO-DAY

— 1913

THE DANCES OF TO-DAY (PART I)

By Evelyn Nesbit Thaw

Is the modern style of dancing really dancing or vulgarity and acrobatics set to music?

You hear the question on every side, with implied criticism of turkey trotting and tangoing in every syllable of the questions.

Modern dancing is really dancing — and I propose to speak in its defense, but I shall divide dancing into two classes, and each class must be kept in its own place. There is stage dancing, which permits of far greater freedom than ballroom dancing should dream of taking. Stage dancing may combine athletics and acrobatics, and even a bit of contortion, all duly mingled with the poetry of motion. Ballroom dancing should be far more conservative — should be, and sometimes is not.

Now, years ago, when the waltz first came into vogue, it had many enemies who considered it vulgar, indecent and well-nigh impossible to allow in respectable places — the poor, dear, conservative little waltz that is allowed by all the people who would scarcely dare to look at a turkey trot to-day!

But the turkey trot is in its infancy — and here be it said that it is a very hale and hearty infant, and when properly

85

brought up and educated will grow into a very charming youth.

I have given time and interest to the study of the modern dance, and through these columns I hope to bring about a better knowledge and understanding of the beautiful steps and postures, the enjoyable motion and gliding that are so much misunderstood and that are maligned, as are all misunderstood things.

The turkey trot and the tango and the better variations of both are beautiful dances in their time and place. But the time is not five in the afternoon, and the place is not the "Dansant" or "Tango Tea."

The Tango Tea is a menace to young girls. Parents who take the proper interest in their children can keep them at home and out of dance halls (spelled with the second vowel if you prefer) at night. But of course young girls have to be allowed a certain amount of freedom in the day, and many a sixteen-year-old child drifts out of the pure air into the drink-and-danger atmosphere of the Tango Tea at five in the afternoon.

Apart from stage dancing, which is meant "for to admire and for to see," there is modern dancing for every one. The place is the home or the private ballroom, and the time is an evening of pleasant relaxation and healthy exercise.

The first thing to consider in ballroom dancing, as I am going to call it, is position. The turkey trot and tango should be danced with the partners a foot apart. These dances must allow for freedom of motion and individual expression, and to be graceful as well as modest they demand room for each partner to move about easily.

First, then, stand a foot apart, with the man's open right palm firmly held at the centre of the girl's waist in back. The girl's left hand is just below the man's right shoulder, with her arm parallel to his; and the girl's right arm is loosely held over the man's left forearm, which is held tense from the bent elbow.

This position allows for free motion and careful guidance that will make for unity of motion without any jerks or jolts. And is not the position modest, even more modest than the now generally accepted and allowed waltz position?

GLIDE ALWAYS

The next great rule for the turkey trotter is: Keep your feet on the floor. Glide, glide all the time; don't bounce or bob, wriggle or sway in the objectionable fashion of people who do not understand the modern school of dancing, but dance at it. Keep your feet on the floor and do not shrug your shoulders; just glide along in a near-walking step — your feet on the floor and your body in a continuous line, with shoulders held even.

Follow the rule as to position, gliding feet and unshrugged shoulders, and at once the objectionable features of the new dance that has swept the country and has given every one the stimulus of enjoyable exercise will be eliminated. But the modern dance is far more than elimination — it is careful selection, and from day to day I am going to show you carefully selected and posed figures and to tell you just how to practice them, so that you may dance with the procession and be a turkey trot and tango expert.

To-day I am showing you a little stretching exercise that it will be wise for you to practice, of suppleness and grace, before you start doing the steps which Mr. Clifford and I will picture for you.

Next consider the tango step, danced for stage purposes only. The step itself is pretty and simple, partners facing forward, man's right and girl's left foot slightly raised, but the close "embracing" position must change for ballroom usage.

The third picture is the best defense I know for the modern school of dancing. Is it not graceful, modest and pretty? I hope soon to teach all of you many steps that belong in just the same category with this step — and I hope that all my long-distance pupils will be able to do steps and whole dances that take their place in the same class with this graceful little near-minuet dip-step.

—AUGUST 16, 1913.

THE DANCES OF TO-DAY (PART II)

By Evelyn Nesbit Thaw

POPULAR opinion is steering a steady course toward a definite goal in its attitude regarding turkey trotting. You remember, of course, the old quotation, "first scorn, then pity, then embrace" — well, that is exactly the course for the turkey trot cup. First horror struck amazement, then amused toleration, then the Everybody's-doing-it-I-must-hurry-and-learn eagerness.

But while everyone is doing it, not everyone is doing it correctly; and the dance of to-day will not come in to its own and rise above popular criticism and accusation, until there is the proper knowledge of how and when and what next.

In a crowded ballroom, if everybody is merely expressing what the music means to them and swaying to the rhythm the dance brings to their own individual minds, there will be bumping and sliding and all sorts of antics that give the satirical writer a chance to liken the dance of to-day to the Moro wooings and the Nautch girl posturings of the back-water civilizations of yesterday.

Last week I gave you three simple rules to fix in your minds before attempting the dances of to-day; stand well away from your partner to allow for individual freedom of motion, keep your feet on the floor to insure gliding instead of hopping, and hold the body — including shoulders — firm and steady.

To-day I want to add an almost equally important rule. Learn your steps and dance them as far as possible with one and the same partner — do this at least until you are sure of yourself; for if every time you dance, you have to readjust yourself to a different sort of guidance, and a new set of steps, you will never master any part of the dance you are trying to learn, but will dance at your goal instead of toward it.

THE TANGO

To-day I am going to give you an idea of the Tango — not the exotic, southern Tango of the Argentine, but a Tango more suited to and more characteristic of our Northern race. They say the Czardas of the Hungarian peasant can be danced in all its perfection by the Hungarian peasant and no other race can compass it. So the Tango Argentina is meant for the man and woman of Castillian blood. With this in view, and with the Tango Argentina as a basis, my dancing partner, Mr. Clifford, has arranged the North American Tango which we introduce in our ballroom dancing at Hammerstein's, and of which I will give you a sketch to-day.

First consider the position — stand with the man's right and the girl's left shoulder almost touching, right and left hands are clasped at waist height and held with unbent arms straight out ahead of the couple whose heads are turned forward and whose bodies are ready for forward motion in the direction of the outheld arms; the man's right arm is at the girl's waist, and her left arm crosses his right as is shown in the first picture.

Now let me add a little secret that makes for graceful dancing of the North American Tango or any other Tango — the girl must lean slightly back and away from the man's supporting arm and her partner inclines forward from the waist.

There are six steps or figures in Mr. Clifford's Tango, which will be found practical and pretty for ballroom dancing; and what is more, I think you will find them easy to master. Always begin a Tango step with the outside foot. Beginning thus, dance forward with arched foot and pointed toe, in stately walking measure for two counts; during the third count the girl turns in to the right, swinging to face her partner, who holds her out at his left side. This step is taken on the girl's right foot, and is followed on the fourth count by a little backward dip on the left foot.

THE REVERSE

Then reverse this step, advancing away from the outpointing hands and then swing back into movement one. Advance and retreat thus eight times, and use each of the other steps. I will describe back and forward thus, eight times in all.

Step two is illustrated by the second picture. Advance with outer foot first, through two counts, on the third give a modest little kicking step as illustrated, and on the fourth count turn to reverse.

Step three is very much like step one except that for a little dip on the fourth count, a deep curtsey is substituted.

Step four is somewhat like step two, but for the kick on count three, a long forward gliding step is substituted — the long glide that is characteristic of the Tango Argentina is here introduced into the North American Tango.

Step five — advance for two counts, and on count three, mark time with the outward foot through two counts, swaying gently while doing this step. The last figure is very pretty and very simple — advance through four counts and turn slowly through four counts, and then do the reverse step away from the outstretched hands for four counts.

The steps may be done forward and in reverse order, or each step may be repeated to the number of four figures of each or eight as I have suggested.

And I do hope that patience, practice, careful following of directions and good music to inspire you will make each of you who read and follow, an expert in the pretty steps of the modest and graceful North American Tango.

—AUGUST 23, 1913.

How to Dance the Tango
By EVELYN NESBIT THAW

The pictures reproduced today, especially posed for this page, show Evelyn Nesbit Thaw's way of dancing the Tango—the kind of Tango she believes to be the best and most graceful variant of the South American dance of that name.

* * * * * * *

This dance, in which Mrs. Thaw has the help of Jack Clifford, she has named the North American Tango, because it is more suited to Northern methods of dancing than its South American namesake.

Next Sunday's Tribune will have a full page article of absorbing interest on the Thaw case, with unusual photographs of Evelyn and Harry Thaw. Don't miss it.

By EVELYN NESBIT THAW
Copyright, 1913: International News Service.

POPULAR opinion is steering a steady course toward a definite goal in its attitude regarding turkey trotting. You remember, of course, the old quotation, "first scorn, then pity, then embrace"—well, that is exactly the course for the turkey trot cup. First horror struck amazement, then amused toleration, then the Everybody's-doing-it-must-hurry-and-learn eagerness.

But while everyone is doing it, not everyone is doing it correctly; and the dance of today will not come into its own and rise above popular criticism and accusation, until there is the proper knowledge of how and when and what next.

In a crowded ballroom, if everybody is merely expressing what the music means to them and swaying to the rhythm the dance brings to their own individual minds, there will be bumping and sliding and all sorts of antics that give the satirical writer a chance to liken the dance of today to the Moro woolings and the Nautch girl posturings of the back-water civilizations of yesterday.

Last time I gave you three simple rules to fix in your minds before attempting the dances of today; stand well away from your partner to allow for individual freedom of motion, keep your feet on the floor to insure gliding instead of hopping, and hold the body—including shoulders—firm and steady.

Today I want to add an almost equally important rule. Learn your steps and dance them as far as possible with one and the same partner—do this at least until you are sure of yourself; for if every time you dance you have to readjust yourself to a different sort of guidance, and a new set of steps, you will never master any part of the dance you are trying to learn, but will dance at your goal instead of toward it.

A NEW WAY TO DANCE THE TANGO

Today I am going to give you an idea of the Tango—not the exotic, southern Tango of the Argentine, but a Tango more suited to and more characteristic of our Northern race. They say the Czardas of the Hungarian peasant can be danced in all its perfection by the Hungarian peasant and no other race can compass it. So the Tango Argentina is meant for the man and woman of Castilian blood. With this in view,

---

Reprint From The Tacoma Tribune, August 1913.

Whipped Cream

Rag

FEATURE NUMBER BEING USED
by
EVELYN NESBIT
and
JACK CLIFFORD

by
PERCY WENRICH

5

Evelyn Nesbit at Hammerstein's in New York, 1913.

PHILOSOPHY

—1914

THE PHILOSOPHY OF EVELYN THAW

By Evelyn Nesbit Thaw

BUT perhaps I ought not to finish without offering you, out of the pages of my diary, written a year or so ago, some scraps of "The Philosophy of Evelyn Thaw." Original and otherwise, they are as follows:

THINGS MANY BLOWS HAVE TAUGHT ME

• In France the men are gallant; in England they are good sportsmen. It means the same, but the gallantry of the Englishman is of a more robust type.

• The most unpopular verse in the Scriptures is, "Let him who is without fault cast the first stone;" it limits the range of criticism.

• Nothing cultivates a sense of honor so assuredly as a big trouble.

• Happy is the woman who can say, "I know the worst that can happen to me — I've had it!"

• The Devil would be blacker than he is painted if a lawyer did the painting.

• Plain women often have plain sailing; pretty women find the sea of life pretty rough.

• If I had my choice whether I would be born beautiful and wicked or plain and good, I should not be born at all.

• If I could live my life over again I would avoid only the follies which had unpleasant consequences.

• Passion is an indication of defective capacity.

• All easy ways are down hill; you don't notice it til you start to climb back.

• Women's steps are hadesward because men are the road-makers.

• A pretty woman who wants work is offered love; a plain woman who wants love gets the darning.

• People always look for a woman in a scandal — there's no need to look for the man; he's in the spotlight all the time.

• Women can live without loving, but not without being loved.

• I think a child is the most terrible happiness life offers.

• Great publics have an infinite capacity for taking the wrong view.

• Modesty has a jumping-off place with every woman.

• Some folks spell "love" with a capital l, and some with a small letter; it is a question of age. I have reached the period of life where I draw a line underneath — just as you do in the case of any other foreign word.

• It is harder to please the low-brow than the high-brow.

• It is always the man who has just jumped on his wife who hisses the loudest at stage villainy.

• It is much easier to be rich than to be strong, and much better to be strong than rich.

• Moderation is a word which has no significance to the idle rich; they play the "no-limit" game, and that's a game in which somebody is surely skinned.

• The way out of life is trouble; the way out of trouble is work.

• It isn't fair to sneer at the virtuous — everybody can't be interesting.

• Temptation is a two-handed game — it requires one player and a dummy.

• Popularity isn't a matter of justice — it's a matter of sympathy. Many a good man or woman deserves popularity who has only respect.

• It's a terrible thing to be respected — it implies such a multitude of "buts."

• A fellow feeling is a term which implies a recognition of one's own weaknesses in others. We have fellow feelings about virtues.

• All the world loves a lover, save one of the lovers' parents.

• The worst thing a woman can do is to do nothing. Nature abhors a vacuum, and the world does not love passive sinners.

• When a woman is faithful to a man people say, "it pays her to be."

• The woman who imputes the worst motives to men is so seldom wrong that she is apt to get swollen-headed.

• Some women are like frosted stone; they repel even the opposite sex by their coldness and harshness. I never see such women with children without marveling how it happened. Other women are like flames — they burn themselves up between lunch and breakfast time.

• Beware of the disinterested man who wants to help you;

pay cash — it will come cheaper in the long run.

• Regrets are useless. You can't repair the foundations from the roof.

• The monk who looked for the Philosopher's Stone and found gunpowder was conducting an experiment which all the women of the ages have been essaying.

• I never regret my life. It would mean regretting much happiness.

• You may do anything in this world so long as you do not reduce your actions to words. Printer's ink is the seal to damnation.

• When a man says a woman is deficient he means that she cannot get down to his level.

*   *   *   *

And here, good friends and enemies, farewell. Think what you please of this, my life. I have told only the truth. But whether you believe it or not makes not an atom of difference to me.

Goodby and good luck to you.

— JANUARY 11, 1914.

EPIGRAMS

— 1927

EPIGRAMS ON BROADWAY

By Evelyn Nesbit Thaw

AFTER an absence of six years, Evelyn Nesbit, ex-wife of Harry K. Thaw, not so young now but still beautiful, is back on Broadway. Miss Nesbit is to manage the Chez Evelyn, a night club at No. 228 W. 52nd St., opening tomorrow night.

Miss Nesbit once ruled with her dancing. Now she is to coach and be proprietor. Rehearsing her bevy of beautiful young blondes and brunettes, she paused yesterday to compare the Broadway she knew with the present Broadway.

¶"Time was when everybody spoke aloud, and even laughed, along the Great White Way — now everyone speaks easy."

¶"If this low talking continues,

97

waiters will have to carry amplifiers."

¶"Oh, yes, Broadway has changed in a million ways. The Cinema and Prohibition did that."

¶"Now we have a Continental Broadway. It is no longer a strictly American Broadway. As our present population demands, now you see there the efficiency of Berlin, some of the gaiety of Paris, and that solid Roast Beef appearance of the Londoner, if you get what I mean."

¶"There are 48 cabarets immediately near 52nd St. and Broadway where I am opening. Forty-eight states of mind may be observed in these places every night. Mine is to be the District of Columbia, as well managed, as prepossessing."

¶"As for the Curfew Law, why that's a child of Prohibition, isn't it?"

* * *

She said yesterday: ¶"I have invited Harry and I think he will probably be there. You know he likes first nights."

— NOVEMBER 14, 1927.

Bibliography
NEWSPAPERS AND MAGAZINES

• *Buffalo Sunday Express**

• *Chicago Evening American**

• *Look Magazine**

• *Motion Picture Magazine**

• *New York American**

• *New York Daily Mirror**

• *New York Daily News*

• *New York Evening Journal**

• *New York Sun**

• *Press Of Atlantic City*

• *San Francisco Chronicle**

• *Tacoma Tribune**

• *Variety*

*out of print.

Bibliography
SOURCES

• *Atlantic City Public Library*

• *Courtroom Warrior* by Richard O'Connor

• *Chicago Public Library*

• *Historic Photos.com*

• *Lancaster Public Library*

• *Library Of Congress*

• *New York Public Library*

• *ProQuest Historical Newspapers*

• *SFX Archive*

• *Sheet Music Consortium*

• *Tacoma Public Library*

• *University Of Arizona Main Library/Special Collections*

Main Street Press • Fort Lee, NJ